D1298623

The Life and Death of a Polish Shtetl

The Life and Death of a Polish Shtetl

Edited by
Feigl Bisberg-Youkelson and
Rubin Youkelson
Translated by Gene Bluestein

University of Nebraska Press
Lincoln and London

This volume was published with the support of
a generous grant from the Cleveland Foundation to
the Department of Religion at Case Western Reserve
University, as part of a project on Jewish-Christian
relations directed by Professors Susannah Heschel
and Eldon Jay Epp.

Library of Congress Cataloging-in-Publication Data
Stshegoye yizker-bukh. English.
The life and death of a Polish shtetl / edited by Feigl
Bisberg-Youkelson and Rubin Youkelson : trans-
lated by Gene Bluestein. p. cm. ISBN 0-8032-6167-5
(paper : alkaline paper)
1. Jews – Poland – Strzegowo-Osada. 2. Holocaust,
Jewish (1939-1945) – Poland – Strzegowo-Osada.
3. Strzegowo-Osada (Poland) – Ethnic relations.
I. Bisberg-Youkelson, Feigl. II. Youkelson, Rubin.
III. Bluestein, Gene, 1928-. IV. Title.
DS135.P62S746713 2000 940.53′18′094384–dc21
99-30394 CIP

For the grandchildren:
Masha Lily, Sarah Jennie, Steven Jacob,
and Isaiah Marley,
so their ancestors will never
be forgotten.

Contents

Translator's Note

This Yizkor, or Memorial Book, for the little town of Strzegowo [STSHE-go-va] was organized and edited by Feigl Bisberg-Youkelson and her husband Rubin Youkelson in 1951. They contacted the contributors and arranged to have the manuscript published, in Yiddish with some parts in English, by New York's Prompt Press as *Strzegowo Yizkor-Book: Commemorating the Town and Community of Strzegowo (Poland), Destroyed and Eradicated by the Nazis.* This first edition included illustrations – photographs and drawings – which unfortunately cannot be reproduced here.

Yizkor is the Hebrew word that means "he shall remember" and also refers to a commemorative prayer for the dead. When I first looked it up to find some historical connections, I was surprised that the current usage, meaning a memorial book, is quite recent. There were a few memorial books published in Europe during the Middle Ages, but Yizkor was not the term used for them. It is in fact a peculiar genre that has been very little researched by lay people or scholars. Around two thousand such studies exist, mostly commemorating the towns of Poland but including also some for towns of other countries and regions (I have found one for the town my mother came from in Bessarabia). And although a collection of remembrances from many different sources has been published, there is only one other translation of an entire book.

My wife's cousin, Aaron Bisberg, first suggested to me that I translate some of these pieces. I was hesitant at first, partly because of the time involved but also because, as the old expression goes, to translate is by definition to betray the originals. I wasn't sure that I wanted to take on that responsibility.

Aaron's concern was that the younger members of the family

should know something about this period in their family's history. Because the book is in Yiddish, they had no chance to read the story. But once I started reading, I couldn't stop. The stories are not only exceptionally well written (the writers are all nonprofessionals), but they tell with great integrity and remarkable candor about the horrors of the Holocaust. Not least are the moving remembrances of what the beloved little town was like before it was invaded by the Nazis.

Though there are many Yizkor books extant, none can be more moving than the one created by the survivors who put this book together with love and tears. I am honored to have established a small relationship with the spirits of these people, who endured the greatest horrors of our times. My sincere wish is that, indeed, they will never be forgotten.

Strzegowo is not an old town. The first inhabitants probably came from Germany, which the town bordered during those days (and probably why it was among the first places the Nazis invaded in September 1939). But there is no documentation for the origins of the people. We can assume they were Ashkenazim, that is, German Jews.

It was not long until Strzegowo was deeply involved in the turmoil of activities that ran through all the Jewish communities in Poland, some of which go back as many as five hundred years. As Feigl Bisberg-Youkelson describes it, she and her friends were all excited by the same important European writers whose works exhilarated many of the young people of the time, from Schopenhauer, Nietzsche, and Kant to Hegel and Marx.

Another major source of interest in the town came from the many Zionist groups who vied for the attention of the people. These ranged from the Orthodox Jews to the Labor or Marxist Zionists, all of whom were preparing to leave for what was then Palestine. (Needless to say those who left were spared from the destruction of the Jews.) Some who left returned, finding the distant country too difficult to settle in, and sadly they joined their neighbors in the tragedy of the Holocaust.

Another major influence among many of the Jews was the Bund – the General Jewish Workers Bund, which was founded in Vilna, Poland, in 1897 and still exists as an organization to this day. Though never under the influence of the Communists, members of the Bund were a strong Socialist group and also major Yiddishists, supporting the work of the many Jewish writers working in that tradition. The Bund was a strong magnet for the radicals in the town; members typically lost interest in it, however, when they arrived in the United States, many shifting their allegiance to the Communist party. (The Bund had never made common cause with the Communists.)

During the war the Bund played a major role in many areas, especially in the Warsaw Ghetto uprising, which it organized with the aid of several left-wing Zionist organizations. Most of the Bund's leaders did not survive.

There are several areas of ambiguity in the following pages. While all the Jews are described as saints, there are some obvious exceptions. One is the rabbi who fell mute on meeting the Nazi commandant and then shortly left the town. (The reader meets him again in the Warsaw Ghetto.) Then there was the unknown Jew who translated the suicide note by Ben-Zion Bogen in what was obviously a traitorous act.

The ghetto was clearly organized by the Nazis, but for several years the Judenrat managed to maintain an almost normal situation. Unlike many Judenräte in Europe, who betrayed their people, the Strzegowo inhabitants appear to have operated sincerely and honestly, until matters passed out of their hands.

Strzegowo was not an entirely Jewish town. There was a sizeable Gentile population which the Jews served as merchants. Before the Nazis the Jews fared rather well. But once the Nazis arrived many Poles acted out the many centuries of anti-Semitism they had grown up with. They became Hitler's willing executioners, as a contemporary author has it.[1] On the whole, most of the Poles behaved as bar-barously as their Nazi contemporaries. Still, as elsewhere in Europe, a small number of righteous Gentiles helped Jews escape from the Nazis, often at their own risk.

Several years ago my wife visited Strzegowo (it has since been re-named Strzegowo-Osada) and discovered that not one Jew has sur-vived. She located the Jewish cemetery on the outskirts of town and saw the monument erected for those hanged by the Nazis. She felt that she was probably the last person who would ever visit it. She attempted to locate the gravestone of her grandfather, but most of the grave markers had been desecrated or overthrown. The only remnant of the village is contained in the following selections.

My wife, Ellie, has been my best reader and editor. I could not have done this work without her help. My son Joel found Strzegowo on the map; my sons Jemmy and Evo provided important help throughout. Ann Baker read the manuscript for the University of Nebraska Press. I thank her for a good close reading. Any errors are my own.

GENE BLUESTEIN
Fresno, 1999

---

1. Daniel Jonah Goldhagen, *Hitler's Willing Executioners: Ordinary Germans and the Holo-caust* (New York: Knopf, 1996). Unless otherwise indicated, all notes are mine.

About the Editors

Rubin Youkelson was a critic and reviewer who wrote for the Yiddish newspaper, *Fraihait*. His wife, Feigl, was a more-than-average housewife and a writer of some skill.

Pronunciation Guide

a as in father	mazl
uh as in above	tuhv (the schwa sound)
e as in egg	veg
ee as in see	byalee
ei as in cradle	Feigl
i as in it	knish
o as in over	oneg shabat
oo as in book	shnook
u as in blue	nu
ai as in aisle	blaiene
oy as in oil	goy
k as in kick	kabuhle
kh	there is no equivalent sound in English but it's like the German *ach*
j as in joy	nooj
r	there are several authentic pronunciations, ranging from a trilled Russian sound to one that sounds like French
s as in sit	nakhis
ts as in fits	tsimis
tsh as in catch	kvetsh
z as in zero	iz
zh as in Zhivago	zhluhb

The Life and Death of a Polish Shtetl

With Bowed Heads . . .

With sad hearts and sorrowful spirits, we begin here the unveiling of this modest memorial – just this Yizkor Book – to commemorate the saintly martyrdom of our slaughtered fathers and mothers, sisters and brothers, comrades and friends from our old home place, Strzegowo.

Only a very few of the Jews in Strzegowo survived the onslaught of the Nazi murderers; only a small number remained to tell the story of the Holocaust. In Strzegowo, as in hundreds of other cities and towns of Poland, there remains not even one Jewish person. Moreover, it has taken us several years after the torrent of Hitlerism to gather the material for this remembrance, this accounting in which we have recorded for future generations the story of martyrdom and heroism concerning the saintly Strzegowo victims.

A town with only a few hundred souls, Strzegowo in the last few decades of its existence undertook to adopt and drink in the social, cultural, and political aspirations of the creative spirit in the Jewish communities of Poland. The little town of Strzegowo was in every way influenced by the cultural advances of its larger neighbors.

This Strzegowo Yizkor Book was created by our own efforts and puts forward a monograph of an annihilated town. At the same time it mirrors something of the lives of Strzegowo townspeople in America and Israel.

Understandably, in much of the book one encounters the tears of mourners; in the reminiscences the tone of eulogy and lament characterize the recalling of the Holocaust. For the sponsors of the book, the memory of the victims of Strzegowo, as well as the entire tragedy of the European Jews, bring forth our special sorrow for those who were nearest and dearest to us.

Let the remnant of all those from the many lost towns in Poland, wherever they find themselves, think of this Yizkor Book as a memorial to all their loved ones, including those mentioned and those whose names are not recalled here.

We want to express here a heartfelt appreciation and thanks to all the townspeople who have sent materials for this book. We are especially grateful to our distinguished fellow townsperson, Yitzkhak Bogen, who fulfilled the arduous mission of describing the background of Strzegowo until the moment of the Holocaust.

For the English-speaking children and relatives of our townspeople as well as for those born in Israel, we printed in English and Hebrew short versions of the meaning of Strzegowo and the mission of this Yizkor Book.

With bowed heads and mournful spirits we stand before this modest memorial to the destruction of the Strzegowo community. "Woe for those who are lost and cannot be recalled." May this Yizkor Book be an eternal memory for the townspeople of Strzegowo and a book of remembrance for all people for generations to come, a testimony to the survival of the Jewish people and their ideals of social justice and world peace to the end of days.

FEIGL BISBERG-YOUKELSON
For the Editorial Committee of the Strzegowo United Relief Committee
September 1951, New York City

IN MEMORY OF STRZEGOWO

While writing these lines, we see before our eyes our brothers and sisters of our birthplace, Strzegowo, who died under torture and in great pain; we hear their last desire unspoken as they left the horrible world:

TELL OF OUR DEATHS! Let not our memory and the memory of our sorrows be forgotten! Let the memory of our martyrdom remain as a head-stone for the few survivors of our city where they may come to weep and recall the tragic loss. And for our people, let it remain as a spark which ignites a great flame of revenge, a constant reminder: erase the remembrance of Amalek . . .[2]

---

2. A traditional name for the enemies of the Jews.

Introduction

This chapter is written mainly for the descendants of the people, the story of whose lives and tragic end make up the contents of this book. To many of the young people who will turn the pages of this Memorial Book and look at the pictures herein, the town of Strzegowo will seem a strange and distant place; and yet these same young people carry part of it in their hearts, characters, and personality makeups, because Strzegowo, its customs, its way of life and spirit, influenced the lives of their parents and their home environments. Indirectly, therefore, there was transmitted something intangible to the young who never saw the town.

The Old Ways

This is the story of a town – a town that lived, created, grew – and perished. It is a part of a set pattern in Jewish history for the past two thousand years: the growth of Jewish communities in some countries and their destruction as a result of political, religious, and social upheavals.

It was a typical small town that grew over a period of years from a small village with dirt roads and unpaved streets, into a community of thousands of people of whom hundreds were Jews.

The economic life of Strzegowo was not all big business. The bulk of the Jewish population consisted of small shopkeepers and artisans, and they eked out a meager existence in the midst of prosperous business activities, which were being carried out through their town.

The commercial phase of life in Strzegowo was predominantly in Jewish hands. They were the business people who supplied the whole population with goods and services.

Introduction

As in all the towns of Poland, religion was a dominating factor in the life of the Jews of Strzegowo. Religion was also the background of education; it began its influence when an individual was born and carried on his education through the old-fashioned "kheder," under the supervision of old scholars whose function it was to indoctrinate the young generation in the precepts of the Torah and the Talmud. From the grownups, daily visits to the synagogue for prayer were expected, and in general, religion was the important and directing force in all situations of life.

The Jewish community had its own court of justice, the rabbi. He used to settle all litigation among Jews by arbitration. He also had the power to grant divorces and to settle various problems within the family. All this led to a way of life that was isolated from the non-Jewish community and explains partly the preservation of customs and traditions and their passing from generation to generation.

Education confined itself solely to the study of Jewish learning. It began early in life, at the age of four, and continued until maturity. There was little secular education available. However, Strzegowo could not resist the trend of the times and new ideas did infiltrate the life of the community. Among these new ideas were primarily Zionism, Poale-Zionism, Bundism, Mizrakhi and others. All the foregone is evidence that Strzegowo was a thriving and intellectually alert little town that mirrored in its confines the strife between progress and backwardness in Jewish life everywhere.

Strange and unpredictable were the ways of fate that prompted some of the Strzegowo inhabitants to emigrate and flee, while others remained to be cruelly destroyed by the Nazis. It is not wisdom, clairvoyance, or superior intelligence that made some people emigrate; neither is it stupidity or backwardness which caused others to remain. Life in Strzegowo held little promise for young people, and consequently the latter were making ceaseless efforts to emigrate; some succeeded in doing so, some did not.

The desire to emigrate did not confine itself to young people only; after the World War it was all-pervading. Anyone of those here in the United States today could have remained over there had not the hand of fate guided them or their parents into the free world many years ago, before the catastrophe was in sight.

The Catastrophe

Because we are unable to present a detailed depiction of the catastrophe that has befallen our unforgettable community Strzegowo, we will just submit some highlights.

On 1 September 1939, the hordes of Hitler swept across from Germany, and within hours were in possession of Strzegowo. The Jews of the town were panic-stricken; they were trapped by the enemy. From their hiding places they watched with fear the goose-stepping Nazis march into Strzegowo. They were trapped by the Nazis, assisted by the local German residents, and there did not seem to be the slightest chance of escaping death.

A reign of terror began immediately. While the Nazis were busy setting up their headquarters, the anti-Semitic Poles went on an orgy of brutality. They, together with the local Germans, dragged the Jews from their hiding places to forced labor, and many of them were murdered. They walked from house to house and did their cruel work. Before the Nazis had time to begin their own program of extermination of the Jews in Strzegowo, some Poles and local Germans gave them a preview of the horrors that would follow.

The Jews of Strzegowo were driven from their homes and herded into a ghetto. A Judenrat was organized to keep order inside the ghetto. The ghetto was very crowded; many families were herded into one room. Privacy and basic comforts were done away with. Yet the Jews did not lose their courage and by a common effort, as if by tacit agreement, carried on even under these terrible conditions. At no time did the Jews of Strzegowo lose their dignity, in spite of the physical degradation and totally abject living conditions.

The policy of the Nazis was to degrade and humiliate the Jews, but in this respect they seldom succeeded. The Jews of Strzegowo never turned against each other; on the contrary they cooperated with one another and shared whatever little they had to the last crumb of bread.

Introduction

A great part of the Jewish community, young and old, died of hunger, sickness, and torture by the Nazis in the Strzegowo ghetto; another part found the same fate in the Warsaw ghetto, while the remaining major part – young and old, men, women, and children – were driven to the concentration camps in Oswiciem [Auschwitz], where they were gassed and cremated by the Nazis in the incinerators. Only a handful – about fifteen in all – remained alive to tell the horrible story of death and destruction.

It follows therefore that everyone of us should consider it a duty to remember those martyrs, our brothers, sisters, parents, cousins, and friends, who did not have the good fortune to save themselves and who perished so horribly. Their memory will live on forever, and this Book is dedicated to the Strzegowo community that was.

No one can deny the law of community in history and civilization; and although the Jewish Strzegowo was erased physically from this world, its spirit together with the spirit of Jewish life in Poland remains an indestructible heritage. This spiritual heritage will live on and perpetuate itself by enriching Jewish life throughout the world.

FEIGL BISBERG-YOUKELSON
[Written in English]

Strzegowo, We Will Never Forget You!

*Facts and Observations Concerning the Establishment
and Accomplishments of the United Strzegowo
Relief Committee in America*

"Strzegowo, We Will Never Forget You!" This is the slogan under which we, in the United State of America, have formed the United Strzegowo Relief Committee. I consider it important that the accomplishments of this organization be recorded in the book we are issuing in commemoration of our little town.

It was in 1946 toward the end of March when my sister Feigl phoned me about a letter she had received from Poland. The letter was dated 11 March. The sender was a man by the name of Fishl Meirantz – a name not familiar to me. Fishl Meirantz had added to his letter a list of the few Jews of Strzegowo who had survived the Nazi slaughter. In his letter he stressed that these survivors were physically and spiritually broken down and in need of immediate assistance.

My sister proposed that we organize a relief committee without delay, that we contact as many of our Strzegowo *landslait* as possible and lose no time in sending aid to the few Jews of our town who have remained alive. My sister told me that she in fact had already begun some small action on her own, but that it was not sufficient. She needed help and wanted to recruit as many *landslait* as could be reached. She thought that I would be the right person to take a serious and active interest in this work.

The next day my sister came over to see me. Before I had an opportunity to say anything to her, she began reading Fishl's letter.

She said, "I hope you understand enough Yiddish."

"Yes," I said, "if you will read slowly."

It was a long letter. Later we had it mimeographed and sent out copies to our *landslait*.

In his letter Fishl described what he had gone through under the Nazis and how his life was saved. He also gave a detailed account of what happened to our friends and relatives in Strzegowo. Not one Jew remained there. Even the cemetery had been desecrated and destroyed.

I listened attentively to my sister's reading. Each time a name was mentioned that she thought I might remember, she would say, "Do you recall him, his wife, his children? They all perished in the crematorium because a Nazi found a piece of bread on one of them."

Many brutal facts were disclosed in Fishl's letter. I was very shaken. I asked my sister to leave the letter with me for several days. We both wept. She gave me the letter and left my office.

Later I once more picked up the letter, and reading it I remembered a great many things of my childhood and the peaceful little town, Strzegowo. So many of us had spent a pleasant youth there. I remembered our chess games, the evening discussions in the library or synagogue. I had a vision of the Saturday afternoons when the young people of the town would go out walking on the highway that led to Mlawa. I thought of many pleasant things. Now it is all gone, destroyed, never to come to life again.

I reached the conclusion that we, the Strzegowo *landslait* in America, can be of help. Although the assistance that we will render might by far not be enough to take care of the needs of our loved ones who survive, yet we will do all that we can. I was convinced of this necessity as soon as it was clear to me what their urgent needs on the other side must be. The question was how to go about helping them. But the answer was simple: we must raise funds, we must give them moral support, encouragement, new hope.

I phoned my sister and told her that she was right, that we must not lose time in setting up a relief organization.

Within two months we already had a list of many names of our landslait. Their response to our first appeal was very encouraging. Some even sent in advance contributions. Our first meeting took place in May 1947 in a New York restaurant. About forty people attended and we raised about $1,000. But no less impressive was the sheer fact of our getting together. Many of us had not seen one another for years. Though the reasons for our getting together were tragic, our reunion was nonetheless a very happy one.

We exchanged memories we had in common, we traveled back to our youthful days in Strzegowo. With deep sorrow we talked about the tragedy of Polish Jewry, the destruction of Strzegowo, as well as the plight of the Jews in general.

At this gathering we decided to name our organization "United Strzegowo Relief Committee." Officers to relieve the temporary committee were N. Novak, P. Stavitzky, and Feigl Youkelson.

Two more important meetings were held, one in November 1947, in the house of Feigl Youkelson in New York City, the other in February 1948 in Philadelphia, in the home of the Steinhauses. Within that short period, we had already managed to send relief to the few from Strzegowo who remained alive and were in Poland, as well as to some who were still scattered, living in the DP camps. As a result of the money we sent to the few remaining Strzegower living in Poland, they succeeded in exhuming twenty bodies of Strzegowo martyrs who were hanged by the Nazis and buried in the desecrated Jewish cemetery. The broken gravestones, too, were reassembled and the cemetery itself fenced off. The committee at that time also planned a project of erecting a memorial monument to Strzegowo and its Jewish martyrs. The monument was to be erected in the old destroyed cemetery. So far, this project, though begun, has not been completed.[3] At the same period, the committee felt that it still was faced with a number of important tasks. To begin with, helping those of our landslait who were still living in the concentration camps to get out and find a new life in Israel, then Palestine, or in our own country, America.

3. The monument was erected at a later date.

Naturally, as our organization continued its work, new problems and new tasks had to be faced.

Approximately every six months a general meeting is held, to which the landslait living in various cities are invited. During the period between meetings, a small committee is functioning, taking care of problems that require immediate attention, such as sending food parcels to Israel or similar things that cannot be postponed until the time of the general meeting.

In the last two years, contact has been established with Strzegowo landslait in Israel, some of whom have lived there for many years, and others who have come there as refugees during the last few years. Simultaneously with these contacts, the idea of a Memorial Book began to take shape. The purpose of such a book is to leave for future generations a documented history of Strzegowo from its early beginnings to the time when Strzegowo, together with hundreds of other Jewish towns in Poland, was wiped off the face of the earth. The book is to be a worthy and dignified monument to those who perished and to their hometowns which were destroyed with them.

As a result of our contact with our landslait in Israel, a Strzegowo relief committee was organized there, too. This was in 1949. It helped us in establishing closer contact with individuals. This contact was strengthened when my sister, Feigl Youkelson, who is the secretary of the Relief Committee, visited Europe and Israel – at her own initiative and expenses – in the summer of 1950. There she helped, primarily through influencing our landslait to write articles from their store of memory and knowledge about Strzegowo, to realize the publication of such a book.

I also want to mention here with gratitude the modest financial contributions of our few landslait in England, whom my sister has visited while in Europe.

In connection with our secretary's visit to Israel, it is worth noting the great joy and interest with which our landslait received her reports from there upon her return. All those present at the meeting felt as if a lost tribe had been rediscovered. A great longing was born within our hearts; feelings that have been latent for many years suddenly came to life again each time Feigl mentioned the names of our *landslait* she had met in Israel.

The greetings she brought were like personal regards from each one there to each one here. Regards from friend and relative to friend and relative. It was, however, also a collective greeting from one community to another, from remnants of a community which once was and now has ceased to exist.

May these three worthy elements – our old memories, the mutual interest, the collective responsibility – help to retain our contact for many years in the spirit and tradition of the old saying: "And a threefold cord is not quickly broken."

JOSEPH BISBERG, *President*

Editor's Note

I am not a native of Strzegowo. The town and its Jewish inhabitants were completely unknown to me until I had volunteered to compile and edit this Memorial Book and until I had read the material that goes in it.

Each manuscript that passed through my hands evoked both profound feelings of sorrow and a deep sense of respect. I saw before me the whole town with its peculiarly interesting characters, its captivating local color, its whole life, which was so brutally destroyed by the Nazi beasts.

There were moments when I felt that each one of the twenty martyrs who were hanged by the Nazis in the little Calvin forest was raising his voice in a bitter, accusing "Why?" "Why has the world permitted it?" Voices shouting for vengeance seemed to well up from all those men, women, and children of Strzegowo who were killed, tortured in the ghettos, gassed and cremated in the death chambers.

As compared with most Jewish towns in Poland, Strzegowo was but a small community of about six hundred Jewish inhabitants. Strzegowo cannot boast of a long history. The Jewish community came to life there only in the beginning of this, our twentieth century. Strzegowo cannot claim to have produced any famous leaders, writers, or artists in any broad sense of the term. The Jewish inhabitants of Strzegowo consisted, with a few exceptions, of workers and artisans who toiled hard for their meager livelihood and were barely able to scrape together enough for *Shabis*. Yet as small as this community was, it had a brisk social and cultural life, its youth was wonderful, and although in miniature form, various organizations and institutions were functioning.

This Memorial Book describes all these facts in a series of impressive articles, some longer, some shorter, written with colorful simplicity and deep honesty. In connection with this aspect of the book I should like to mention with appreciation the esteemed Reverend Itzkhak Bogen, one of the first pioneers of the Jewish settlement in Strzegowo and now for many years a resident of Israel. His article about the birth and development of Strzegowo describes the very beginnings of its Jewish community.

I should also like to express my appreciation at this point to Joseph Rosenberg, also a resident of Israel, for his semi-fictional story in which he so lovingly and heartily describes a whole gallery of interesting characters in Strzegowo.

The above-mentioned contributions gained in strength and impact by the various shorter articles, memoirs, episodes, and adventures by other contributors from Strzegowo. Together these descriptions grow into a colorful, vigorous portrayal of all that was characteristic of this town, its social activities, its joys and sorrows, its hard life, its eternal hopes.

Of special value are the articles dealing with the destruction of Strzegowo, written by the few who have survived.

I wish to point out specifically the contributions of Fishl Meirantz, Ben-Zion Bogen, Hinde Berlin, and Molly Piotrikowsky. With a great deal of detail, they describe the grueling acts of the Nazis and their local henchmen: how they began their bloody work and with what bestiality they carried out its murderous conclusion.

The shorter descriptions by Israel Silberstrom, Beinush Vure, and others are valuable contributions and important supplements to the history of the destruction of Strzegowo.

Of no less value are the other articles, including two written in Hebrew, by Itzkhak Tanditsharzen and Joseph Rosenberg (those articles are of special value to the Sabras in Israel), as well as the compact compilation of material in English for the Americans born of Strzegowo descent. They are all important additions to the history of Strzegowo, of its life and brutal destruction.

Very valuable and deeply moving are the few photographs of the exhumed bodies of the twenty Jewish martyrs who were hanged by the Nazis. They were buried in the desecrated ruins of the Jewish cemetery – a cemetery which in itself stood out like a lone tombstone in memory of Strzegowo and its inhabitants, of a life that was and no longer is.

Unstinted recognition for the sacred work of exhuming the martyrs should be given to the survivors, Fishl Meirantz, Avreml Pinkert, Yeshaye Margolin, Beinush Vure and Sanek Plot. With the aid of the American landslait, the above-named individuals have also restored the cemetery, have fenced it off and erected a monument on the bruder-keiver of the twenty martyrs.

Expressing thanks to all those who have contributed in writing and with photographs for this book, I wish to express the greatest thanks to my dear wife, Feigl (Bisberg-Youkelson). She not only was the initiator of the idea for this book, but has invested superhuman work to organize the difficult project and helped to realize it.

She has written scores, perhaps hundreds of letters to landslait in America, Israel, France, England, Poland, and during the first few years to those who were still in the concentration camps of Germany and the DP camps of Austria and Italy. In her letters she demanded material for the Memorial Book. She encouraged writing and outlined what to write about. Of special significance was her contribution in connection with a trip to Europe and Israel in 1950. There she personally influenced many landslait and old residents of Israel as well as new arrivals, to write for this book.

Aside from this basic work, Feigl has been of great help in assorting the material, gathering photographs, giving advice, and generally assisting in the compilation of the book. Without her energetic, untiring efforts, it would have been impossible to even think of a Strzegowo Yizkor Book.

This modest Memorial Book, dedicated to the memory of the tiny Jewish community of Strzegowo, is a valuable addition to a long list of similar books, dedicated to other destroyed Jewish towns and cities. These memorial books occupy a unique place in the voluminous memorial literature in which, through poems, novels, plays, documentary books, etc., the greatest catastrophe in Jewish history, a catastrophe in which six million Jews have been exterminated, has been recorded and immortalized.

These Yizkor Books will serve future historians as an important source from which to draw factual information, not only about the unprecedented destruction in the era of Hitler, but also in regard to many Jewish towns and cities and their inhabitants.

Our Memorial Book, which was created with tender piety, with sadness and grief, we bring to our Strzegowo *landslait* as well as to the Jews throughout the world as our modest monument to the incomparable pain and heroism of those people who have perished in Strzegowo: a monument for all future generations.

With this book another bloody chapter is added to the greatest tragedy that befell our people – the extermination of one third of the Jewish people and of countless Jewish communities. Through this Memorial Book, in the name of those who left no written testament, we hurl our curse at the Nazis and their fascist followers the world over – a curse to the Nazis and a demand and a warning to those of our present as well as future generations, to be on the alert and never again permit a repetition of such monstrosities.

Yizkor – in memory to the martyrs.

Yizkor – as a reminder of our duties and obligations to hold their legacy sacred.

RUBIN YOUKELSON
New York, September 1951

The Founding and Development of Jewish Strzegowo

*Preamble to a Study from Israel a Year after
the Founding of the State*

With a heart full of woe and tears in my eyes, I bring here a short overview of our dearly beloved little town, Strzegowo – may its memory be blessed. It needs to be said that even if all human beings were writers and all the waters of the earth were ink, it would still not be possible to describe and illustrate the greatness and significance of our little town. You might very well ask: "How can anyone exaggerate its importance to such an extent?" To which I reply: "Although it was small in quantity, it was nonetheless great in quality and bearing, deserving of praise without limit."

As a further confirmation of the truth of my assertion, the fact needs to be underscored that the entire history of our little town, from its founding to its extinction, is less than a Jubilee – fifty years. When we look at the rich content, the core of its Jewish life, the way it developed, and the heights that were achieved, the prestige of Strzegowo surpasses proportionately even those towns that have existed for many more years. So how can one possibly forget such a dear little town with its great and beautiful virtues? No, we can never forget that. It remains an eternal memory. And in view of all this, we need to pause for a moment, think deeply, meditate seriously, and say: "Think what happened to us – may the souls of the people be bound up with the Lord in the bond of everlasting life."

There once was a town called Strzegowo near Mlawa, Poland, at that time under the control of Czarist Russia. The town was split in two by a river called Jahlduovka [Wkra], which flowed from Jahlda,

Germany, to Wkra and beyond, where it emptied into the Vistula. There was a bridge over the river.

About fifty years ago [in 1896] the Czarist government issued an edict that a hundred and one villages should be known as towns. That is to say, each one was to institute a market day once a week and once every eight weeks a one-day fair. As a result little Strzegowo became a town.

The Czarist regime also ordered that on the market day a doctor from the nearby town of Shrensk would be available for the people of Strzegowo and neighboring environs. According to the government's decree, a sick person had to pay twenty groshn for each prescription. The visit of the doctor motivated the people from neighboring villages to come to town on market days. Another important factor in the influx of people was the fact that there were a great many side roads in nearby towns like Mlawa, Tchekhenov, Ratshoynu, Plinsk, Shrensk, and Drobin, roads that led to Strzegowo. That was relatively unusual in those times. So that was why the town began to develop very quickly.

On the market days a great number of peasants started coming from nearby areas, and because of that there were very large market days. Many merchants from neighboring towns also came, and there developed a large trade in horses, large animals, pigs, poultry, and household goods, with a special spot in the marketplace for each of the various items. As a result, Strzegowo became a place of extensive trading and a good place to make a living.

As I mentioned earlier, Strzegowo was divided by a river. The majority of the Jews lived on the side where the road led to Mlawa. That was also where most of the commercial activity took place. The other side, which led in the direction of Ratshoynu, was inhabited by a small Gentile community and perhaps ten Jewish families. The church was also in that location. The Jews came to pray at the home of Yitzkhak Rosenberg, of blessed memory, the *shoykhet* [the person officially authorized to slaughter animals according to Jewish law]. The area where the first group of Jews was settled, in the direction of Mlawa, was originally a forest owned by a local landowner.

In the very beginning when the Jewish community began developing, there was only a small cluster of Jewish families, of which some of those described here came from nearby villages. Among those involved was Aaron Bisberg.

Around that time [in 1902] there arrived Itche Meir Piotrikowsky, who had been involved in business activities in Radzhimovits, which was not far from Strzegowo. He then bought the land from the owner and began chopping down the trees to provide an area for the development of Strzegowo's Jewish community. At that time, I, Piotrikowsky, and his nephew arrived. In that same area, the marketplaces of Strzegowo began to develop. Also the landowner began selling small sites near the forest to Jews who began to establish themselves there.

After a few years the wife of the landowner decided to bring a suit against the Strzegowo people and the outside merchants. It was her contention that the market belonged to her. She claimed that she had not sold the market itself, only the area around it. The trial went on for quite a while but in the end she won her case. All of the merchants who used the market had to pay her a fee. Then the government bought her out and began to collect the money.

In the meantime, Gentiles began purchasing pieces of land in the area near the Jewish community and Jews began to build many different kinds of stores. In that way a significant Jewish community was developed in Strzegowo where there was a great deal of commerce, mainly in Jewish hands.

Strzegowo Gets a New Name – New Berlin
Suddenly, at one point, Strzegowo was given a new name. People started referring to it as "New Berlin." That particular nickname was never officially proclaimed by anyone and was never written in any record books. The name "New Berlin" was developed for the following reasons: since a beautiful town was quickly developed out of some sandy lots, which were turned into places of business where one could make a living; and where there was a locality that pulsated with life and capabilities; and since there began to develop

vital institutions; consequently people began referring to the area as a "Novy Berlin."

I actually don't recall, but my wife remembers that when Jews got together, they were in the habit of using the name "New Berlin," and the usage was spread to the Gentile community as well. For several years the name persisted, but since the official name of the town remained Strzegowo, the title "New Berlin" gradually disappeared and was finally forgotten. The Jewish people in Strzegowo never had their own official community status but were placed under the jurisdiction of Radzhinow. The people of Radzhinow demanded fees for all official functions that were required to be performed. Consequently, the Jews in Strzegowo were dependent on Radzhinow for all community requirements, such as recording births, marriages, divorces, and deaths. And even the burials were done in the Radzhinow cemetery.

When Yitzkhak Srebrenik came to Strzegowo in 1904 as town rabbi, the people began to work toward achieving status as an independent community. That required the agreement of the government and the legislature in Mlawa. Finally, after a good deal of negotiation between the two groups, Strzegowo was officially declared to be an independent polity with all the rights that were necessary. At that point, Itche Meir Piotrikowsky donated a piece of land to serve as the home of a Jewish city council. At the same time Pincus Piotrikowsky, the father of Itche Meir, died, and since it is not allowed to leave just one grave in a cemetery, a tomb was built for the first occupant of a grave in the Jewish cemetery.

It's hard to remember the names of those who came early and those who came later to settle in Strzegowo, so perhaps the best way to do it is alphabetically. [There follows a long list of names.] In addition to those names, there were also those who were born in the town, so that by the 1920s there were approximately six hundred souls in Strzegowo.

The town grew and developed with love from one to another, without concern whether one was orthodox or progressive and regardless of the variety of political positions in the town. A few years later, when Itche Meir Piotrikowsky bought the mill and a good parcel of land round it, he also built a synagogue and a mikve [a ritual bathhouse] at his own expense and hired a young man according to the ancient custom, who was given room and board for his services. In 1904 Yitzkhak Srebrenik was hired as rabbi and given a place in the home of Itche Meir. The townsfolk of Strzegowo, both the Jews and Gentiles, were very much influenced by the highly virtuous behavior and approaches of Itche Meir. Moreover, his generosity in making such donations had a wide appeal and even carried over to other villages and towns in Poland. The feeling of unity among the Jewish townspeople was best revealed during the Jewish holidays.

Strzegowo especially distinguished itself during the time of World War I when half of the Jewish community in Mlawa was forced to flee the city, which was near the German border. They were received by the people of Strzegowo with the deepest warmth and brotherly love. Every household took in a few families – each according to its ability – without any sense of being compensated. Such a truly humanitarian approach among the Jews even had a strong impact on the Gentile community. Even the priest, Grochowsky, who was widely known as a notorious anti-Semite when he served as the priest in Ratshoyniz, was greatly moved by the high moral tone that prevailed in the town and made attempts to befriend the Jews, and indeed showed it in his deeds. I'll illustrate the truth of this with further examples later on.

The Social Life of Strzegowo

The Jewish community began to install necessary social institutions such as, for example, a hospital, a group to visit the sick, a study group, a woman's organization, and other similar groups.

Also at this time opinions began to develop about various political parties and ideological points of view, including many Zionist parties as well as the Bund.[4] All of these developed their own activi-

4. An influential Jewish socialist organization that strongly opposed Zionist appeals for relocation to what was then Palestine.

ties in accordance with their special interests. At the same time there was a jointly-sponsored library and a drama circle. In either the library or the drama circle, there were opportunities for all to participate regardless of their political convictions.

It's noteworthy that despite the fact that the young people had their own political and cultural organizations, when the holidays came around they did not isolate themselves from the communal life of the Jewish community but rather took part in the celebrations, especially during the High Holidays and Simkhas Torah.

In later years there were organized two different kinds of children's schools, one called the House of Jacob (especially for girls) and another specialized school, in addition to the already existing kheders and Talmud Torahs. After World War I it was apparent to many of the young people that they had no secure future in Strzegowo, or in Poland generally, and they began to wander away from the town, some to the United States, some to Cuba, Argentina, Mexico, and then later to what was then called Palestine.

Some Characteristic Scenes from Jewish Life in Strzegowo

I recall that when the Jewish community in Strzegowo began to develop and started thinking about hiring a rabbi for the town, I and Simkhe Joel Plaut, with the permission of the people, traveled as a delegation to Dronin, where there lived a great Talmudic scholar, Yitzkhak Srebrenik, who was well-qualified to take the position of rabbi. Rabbi Srebrenik approved of our plan, and we returned to the town with him. I remember that he was wearing the traditional "Jewish hat," which was not appropriate for a rabbi, so I changed it to one more fitting.

The town greeted the new rabbi with honor, and Itche Meir Piotrikowsky provided him with a room in his house, where the rabbi promptly installed himself. As part of the arrangements for him, the people gave the rabbi the exclusive right to sell leaven, a procedure common in all the little Jewish towns at that time. Even some of the Gentile bakeries bought their leaven from the rabbi.

It was also established as an ongoing custom that during the Jewish holidays the people of the town used to assemble at the rabbi's house and make a solemn pledge to him. In another nice tradition the heads of the households used to show their respect for the rabbi and the *shoykhet* during the holidays.

From the time that Rabbi Srebrenik became the town rabbi and for several years thereafter, Strzegowo was still under the jurisdiction of the Radzhinow Jewish community. One day shortly after Rabbi Srebrenik was appointed rabbi for the town, Yehuda Leib Rosenblum, the rabbi from Radzhinow, came to Strzegowo and complained about the fact that the Jews of the town had set their own independent rabbinate. As a result there developed a quiet conflict between the two rabbis.

This antagonism could be seen in the following peculiar circumstances: both rabbis officiated that Saturday in the same synagogue; both recited all of the most holy prayers and the prayers for Sukkoth; and each delivered his own sermon. The winner of the conflict was Rabbi Srebrenik, who had the majority of people in the Jewish community in Strzegowo behind him. And the powers that be also decided that Strzegowo was qualified to become independent in these matters. The rabbi's reputation continued to develop and had an impact in other communities as well. When the rabbi of a neighboring town died, Rabbi Srebrenik was called to preside over their future decisions.

As is well known, rabbis and great scholars used to travel from town to town delivering sermons. Among those who came to Strzegowo once was Rabbi Jacob Solomon Simyatitsky, who excited the whole community with his inspired sermons. He was so impressive that the community immediately nominated him to become the town's rabbi. He was also highly capable in ritual services and inspired the people with his prayers. He had the honor of maintaining the rabbinate in Strzegowo until the last days, when the Nazi troops of bitter memory fell upon the town. Rabbi Simyatitsky died in the Warsaw ghetto. May his soul be bound up with the Lord in the bonds of everlasting life.

Strzegowo Organizations

The Strzegowo city organizations, the police, the doctor, even the priest, were all very friendly to the Jews. The general bank of Strzegowo was organized by Jews and Gentiles together. The Gentiles deposited their money in the bank, and the Jews loaned it out. When the vote was taken, the Gentiles all agreed that Itche Meir Piotrikowsky should be the chairman of the bank. Later, when Itche Meir retired, the post went to the priest, Father Grachowsky, and Eliezer Gips. It was understood by everyone that the real director was Gips. I recall once when I was in need of a loan of eight hundred zlotys and it happened to be on a Sunday, Eliezer Gips went to see the priest, who was wearing his ritual clothing. The priest changed into his everyday clothes and went down to the bank so that I could get my money right away.

Here is another interesting episode: there was an incident in which the director of the Polish school insulted one of the Jewish children. The Jews called a meeting to discuss what should be done. The director came to the meeting, apologized for the affair and promised that it would never happen again.

Jews from Strzegowo in Palestine

As to the attitudes toward Palestine in Strzegowo, there were at the time various opinions and points of view, as indeed there were throughout Poland. After World War I, there was a strong attraction on the part of a considerable number of Jews in Strzegowo to emigrate to Palestine. So Itche Meir Piotrikowsky traveled to Palestine three times and sent messages back to the publication, The Jewish Word, describing the way of life there at that time. Later Abraham Cooperman, the son-in-law of the *shoykhet*, left for Palestine and became the head of a school in Tiberias. Some years later, Eliezer Gips and his whole family left for Palestine. On the occasion of his leaving, the whole town turned out to honor him and wish him well. Abraham Binam Margolin greeted him while mounted on a white horse, which gave the occasion a special quality. All the Jews made clear their wishes that he should establish the way for all the others to follow. Unfortunately, Eliezer Gips was not successful and it was necessary for him to return to Poland, where he went under with all the other victims of the Hitler murderers. While in Palestine he married off his oldest daughter and because of that three other of his children went to Palestine as well. His son, Moyshe, the only one who survived the Holocaust, went to Israel in 1945. Some time earlier, after World War I, Ben-Zion Laskrits and also I and my family and some others also went to Israel. So at the moment there are between sixty and seventy souls from Strzegowo living in Israel.

The Destruction of Strzegowo

Luckily, at the time of the destruction of Strzegowo I was long gone. That tragic moment of terror and pain is described by the few survivors in other portions of this book. My heart trembles at the thought of the terrible fate of our unforgettable little town and the rest of the Jewish people in Poland.

I want to take this opportunity, in closing, to recall the memory of my loving daughter and her husband, my two grandchildren, my two loving sisters and their families, may their souls be bound with the Lord in the bonds of everlasting life. May God bless the souls of all the people of Strzegowo and all my relatives and the saintly victims who were killed, strangled, burned, hanged, for the Holy Name. May the Lord avenge their blood.

YITZKHAK BOGEN, 1946

Three Unforgettable Proper Ladies from Strzegowo

Among the many different types of people that come to mind when I think back about our beloved little town, Strzegowo, which disappeared as a Jewish community, three particular women come to mind, each of whom embodied typical qualities of the women of their time. Their character traits were symbolic of the world outlook of the generation that existed in the period before the accursed Hitlerites.

I'd like to describe briefly the unique qualities of each of these proper ladies: Mama Rachel (the wife of Nathan Isaac Plaut), Yente the Rebbitsn (the wife of Mendl Borenstein, the school teacher), and Sarah-Vita (the wife of Aaron Bisberg).

These were three women from the older generation in Strzegowo. They were truly three pillars of the community, with persistence in their religious habits, each in her own way.

Mama Rachel

Mama Rachel was almost six feet tall, with very pale skin, a round face, and alert, brown eyes. She wore a fashionable wig – in a word, she was a lovely woman who evoked reverence and respect.

Mama Rachel had eight children, only one of whom [a seventeen-year-old son] died. Everyone in the town called her Mama Rachel and she earned the title legitimately. For one thing, she religiously observed all of the orthodox requirements. For some time she was in charge of the *mikve*. Like a real mother, she paid attention to all the problems that arose and was especially attentive to the younger women, whom she tried to steer in the right direction.

Later on she was the manager of the Strzegowo inn on the road to Mlawa where all the wagoners from neighboring towns used to stay. She was a great cook, and everyone complimented her on her culinary abilities. And just as she was a great cook, she was also known as a wonderfully competent housewife. Her own house was known to be exceptionally and immaculately clean.

Although there was in Strzegowo a traditional barber-surgeon, Mama Rachel often took over his duties.[5] Whenever a child or an adult became ill, Mama Rachel was often called to help the sick patient.

I recall that when I was a child and had a sore throat, she put me on her knees and swabbed my throat unmercifully. Although it was terribly painful, I didn't utter a peep. And when she was done, she gave me a kiss and said: "Now you will feel better."

Mama Rachel also delivered the children for poor women, like a real midwife. And if a Jewish woman died, Mama Rachel was the one who washed the body, prepared it for the Last Judgment, measured the body, and sewed the burial shroud. As a consequence of all these capabilities, Mama Rachel was celebrated as a beloved person in the Strzegowo Jewish community. She will never be forgotten.

Yente the Rebbitsn

Yente got her name because she was religious to the point of fanaticism. Since she was rather heavy, she was also known as "Yente, the Chubby One." She kept herself meticulously neat and tidy. She always wore an apron that covered not only the upper part of her body but went down far below her knees.

She wore a head covering that almost concealed her face and was more beautiful than any other in town.

Yente the Rebbitsn was also capable of being a teacher and could read even the smallest characters of text. And when her husband,

5. The barber in many a European small town was also capable of performing minor surgery and especially applying *bankes*, the small round glass cups that were placed on the back or chest to cure various illnesses. The Yiddish word is *feldsher*.

Mendl, one of the Hebrew teachers in town, was ill and could not meet with his students, she was competent to take his place. She was also the spokesperson for the women's section of the synagogue, interpreting for those who could not read Hebrew. The women thought of her as an especially holy person, since it was through her that they could come into contact with God. Whenever she spoke a prayer, the women imitated her and repeated the words. As a result, there were often some comical occasions.

So, for example, if she ever said something in between intoning the prayers, the women would mechanically repeat it even though it had nothing to do with praying.

Yente the Rebbitsn, like Mama Rachel, was one of the key personalities among the women of Strzegowo. And Yente the Rebbitsn also remains unforgettable.

Sarah-Vita, the Wife of Aaron – My Mother

My mother, Sarah-Vita, was born in Mlawa. She was the only one of eleven children who remained alive. Her father, Moyshe, died at a very young age. The name Vita was added to Sarah because it means life [in Latin], and it was in hopes of giving her longevity. Because she was so poor, she was brought up in the home of a relative, Mendl Domb, who was also a Talmudic scholar. And since she grew up in such a religious atmosphere until her marriage, she soaked in a great many religious habits that lasted throughout her life. My mother, Sarah-Vita was physically a very weak person, but she was spiritually very robust.

After World War I, when Mendl Domb stayed in our house for a few months, he used to refer to Sarah-Vita as a saintly person. A friend from Mlawa, Mytl Landis, also used to refer to her the same way.

My mother was so deeply religious that she used to pray three times a day and also read regularly in a number of religious books. She actually had a collection of some rare religious volumes, which she guarded carefully. And she knew a good number by heart. When it came to discussions of religion, she was rarely behind the times.

Her religious habits expressed themselves also in humane behavior. For example, on Friday nights she sent each of her children to a poor family that was not able to celebrate the Sabbath adequately. To one she gave some fish to deliver, to another child some chicken, and to yet another *khale*. She behaved this way for two reasons: first, to raise the spirits of poor families and enable them to celebrate the Sabbath appropriately, and second to acquaint her children with the requirement to bring the necessities for the Sabbath to those in need. Like my mother, my beloved father also had the same habits and behaved in the same humane way.

It was a tradition that on the Sabbath there was always a guest invited to our table. My mother rarely ever cooked only enough for our family even on weekdays, but always made sure that there would be enough for a few extra people. She was a specialist in entertaining guests. The door to our house was always open to everyone.

I remember once when my mother became gravely ill. Almost everyone in the town was ready to take part in efforts to save her life.

Of her five children – three sons and two daughters – the oldest, Joseph, was her favorite. When he got married and left for America, it was a great blow to her. That was especially because while he was in Strzegowo, Joseph clearly was traveling in her footsteps. Even strangers felt blessed by him.

After World War I, when my father died and my mother was left responsible for the children, Joseph was determined to bring his mother to America. Although she was not anxious to go to America because she knew that it would be difficult to keep her religious observances there, she agreed nonetheless because the proposal had come from her beloved son, Joseph. When she arrived she was very disappointed as she realized how commercialized religion had become here. She even lost her enthusiasm for the spiritual leaders of the community, and she tried to go her own way and keep up the traditions she had observed in Strzegowo. Her children saw to it that she was not hindered in her practices and that she should live her own life as she saw fit. She was so devoted to her habits that she refused to eat meat or butter; she ate poultry only when she could see that the *shoykhet* had ritually done the slaughtering and she could add her own prayers. As a result of her strict observances, she was unable to live either with her children or anyone else.

In 1946 my mother died at a ripe old age, symbolically on Mother's Day, the occasion in America when mothers are honored by their children.

May these words be the memorial from her children to the brilliance of her life.

FEIGL BISBERG-YOUKELSON
New York

The Strzegowo Campsite

Almost every small town in Poland had a rich natural habitat that was especially nourishing to its youth. Strzegowo was no exception.

Strzegowo established the campsite, a rich natural treasure for the Jewish youth. The campsite, a half-mile from the town, consisted of hills with many trees and valleys festooned with flowers through which a crystal-clear stream flowed, the overflow of the Zholduvka River. The river provided not only a refreshing and meditative aspect to the place; it also provided a convenient location for the people to bathe. The men were on one side and the women on the other. The partition between them consisted of bushes and trees. The women bathed in their nightdresses, and the men bathed in the nude. When a man intentionally or accidentally wandered into the women's area, you could hear the shrieks of the women all around the place, cries from chaste and naive maidens with turbulent emotions.

During the winter the *shoykhet*, Abraham Yitzkhak Rosenberg, used to chop a jagged hole in the ice and immerse himself as if he were in the *mikve*. He was a person with a strong constitution.

Among the campsite's special qualities was one that endeared itself especially to the mothers of the town. That was the white sand that was used to clean the floors and the houses in honor of the Sabbath and holidays or when special guests were expected. Children were sent to the campsite with sacks and little shovels to gather the sand and bring it home. It's noteworthy that the deeper they dug, the whiter the sand they unearthed.

The campsite was the basic spot for romantic and studious youth, for the intellectual crowd. I remember personally many moments when I had read a book that made a great impression on me, and I had the need to share my impressions with one of my friends. I used to grab one of my comrades, mostly Sheintshe, the *shoykhet's* daughter, and run to the campsite where we could go over the book and discuss it fully. I remember also that when I was a member of the youth section of the Bund (and caught up in the movement), a bunch of us young people used to go to the campsite to celebrate the first of May, May Day. The occasion was marked by readings about the meaning of this workers' holiday, with quotations from Karl Marx.

I remember once going to the campsite with a young man and suddenly becoming terrified that the spell of nature would overpower my girlish modesty, although for dates there was an even better place in Strzegowo. That was the great orchard that was part of the German borderland. In that orchard there were many different kinds of fruits and flowers; each spot had its own special trees and flowers and everywhere there was a charming nook for spooning.

There, as in the campsite, young people were enveloped by a sweet dream of romance that, for many of us, was still a mysterious interlude.

O my dearest campsite! The most beautiful moments of our youth are entwined with you. And now at this time when we recall our beloved Strzegowo, let us also shed a tear for your memory as well.

Feigl Bisberg-Youkelson

Sheindele, the Gem of Strzegowo

To the Memory of Sheindl, the Shoykhet's Daughter

The house of the *shoykhet* was an unusual place in our Strzegowo. The father, Avrom Yitzkhak, never raised his voice in anger and the mother, Rivkele, was like a gentle dove emanating modesty, love, and tenderness. The children never feared their parents and showed them great respect. The home was a lesson in harmony and family love.

In such a house, in that atmosphere, Sheindl was born and reared and became a bright and loving person. Sheindele played the violin, learned how to read music, and wrote poetry. In short, Sheindele was a colorful, humane presence – the gem of Strzegowo.[6]

Sheindl dreamed of life in the great world. Although she dearly loved Strzegowo, at the same time she felt hemmed in by it. As fate would have it, however, she was never to leave Strzegowo.

After I left for America in 1921, I carried on a regular correspondence with the beloved friend of my youth. It's no exaggeration to say that every one of her letters was filled with highly intellectual content; she recalled there our youthful studies together, reading the important works of philosophy and social history – Nietzsche, Schopenhauer, Kant, Hegel, Babel, Forel, and others, including Yiddish, Polish, and world literature.

After Sheindl was already married to Moyshele, the husband of her dead sister, Gitele, she wrote once to say: "I would like very much to come to America." I talked this over with my brother, Volf [Bill], and he immediately began to make plans to bring Moyshele

6. Throughout this piece, Feigl plays on the connotations of Sheindl: brilliant, gem-like.

over, even preparing some of the necessary papers. But Sheindele would not agree that Moyshele should come first and then bring the whole family. As a result, the proposal to come here was not carried out.

And so Sheindele and her husband and children remained in Strzegowo, where they were all murdered by the Nazi butchers. This memoir of my unforgettable, beloved childhood comrade is sealed with hot tears – Sheindele, the *shoykhet's* daughter, the gem of Strzegowo.

FEIGL BISBERG-YOUKELSON

My Town Strzegowo,
as I Remember It

I remember the beautiful little town of Strzegowo, where my parents were married, where all my brothers and sisters were born, where we used to ramble over the green hills and swim in the lovely lakes, where we used to play in its gorgeous campsite, where we lived in friendly relations with all of our neighbors. All these wonderful pastimes remind us of how our childhood was spent.

When summer came I remember swimming in the lake with an apron instead of a bathing suit. I recall that at around four in the morning, Joseph Bisberg used to come to our house where my father studied some pages from Gemara with him. My father admired Joseph and loved his yearning to know more and more about the Talmud. But, oy! How the peculiar sing-song of the studying kept the rest of us from sleeping!

And then there was winter. I recall the early mornings at the Bisberg's house when we used to wake up shivering with cold and Sarah-Vita, with special attention to each of us, would set out those heavenly blue porcelain cups full of hot tea and milk. And next to each cup was a little lump of sugar. How delicious and tasty it was! It started the day just right.

And then there was the school, run by Urish, which consisted of one room where we learned to write [Yiddish and Polish] and also studied arithmetic. I could never keep up with Feigl in arithmetic.

Urish was an unusual person. He was polite and courteous and had a warm, friendly manner. He was formerly a soldier in the Czarist army. When we saw him in the street, we used to curtsey and speak amiably. It was different in the Hebrew school, where the teacher, a man with a long beard, had a habit of pinching the girls' behinds and beating the boys with a whip. There was another teacher who never hit anyone but smelled awfully of onions.

I also remember Mondays. Monday was the market day and the whole town was excited: peasants from the nearby villages, merchants from neighboring towns came to Strzegowo with all kinds of products – grains, vegetables, poultry, homemade crafts. The day was full of commerce and dealing. My mother sold butter and eggs and I sold *kvass*, which I kept in a bucket of ice and sold for a penny a glass. No one could afford to buy a whole bottle.

I liked to watch the Jewish housewives when they came to the market to buy chickens, feeling and pinching the chickens to see if they had any eggs in them or if they were fat enough to provide *shmalts* for Passover. And how my mother took the risk of selling saccharine illegally, while Goldzhkin, the only cop with a human attitude, used to shield my mother when he was occasionally ordered to arrest her.

And then there were the Sabbath days. They began Friday afternoon when the housewives used to start chopping onions and all the other things that were required for the gefilte fish. Over the whole town you could hear the rhythmic sounds of cleavers against their cutting boards. From every house there came the deliciously charming odor of fresh *khale* and other baked goods and the smell of chicken soup. Also on that day the *tsholnt* was prepared and left to bake in the hot oven over night. And who can forget how we used to run to the bakery for braided *khales* and other Sabbath delights for the *tsholnt*. Wonder of wonders – the Bisbergs had their own baking oven in which they baked everything in their own house! We had to carry the *tsholnt* to the baker, David Siskind.

Yes, the Sabbath was the most beautiful day in the week. Everyone dressed in their finest clothes and, with the parents at the head, marched in a procession with dignity and respect to the small but impressive synagogue for the Sabbath services. On Saturday afternoon we young girls used to gather at the home of our friends to celebrate together, each one bringing candies, baked goods, and other snacks. And on Saturday evenings, after our mother passed away and our father left for America, we were homeless and loved to spend time in Sarah-Vita Bisberg's house. We watched every week, wide-eyed with excitement as the *shoykhet* slaughtered an animal, removing the innards, especially the milt [spleen]; then Sarah-Vita would prepare a huge portion of giblets. We all knew that we would share some of that feast the next day. It was our best meal of the week.

Now I recall Passover, especially the day before the holiday. Everyone was excited and full of holiday spirit. Feigl, Rachel, and the other girls of the village used to run back and forth to the river to scrub the troughs, the rolling pins, and the noodle boards in order to erase any vestige or sign of *khoomits* [leavened dough]. Every house was involved in the same task and had its own little mound of dishes and household furnishings piled up at the entry to the house. The small buckets of water that were usually brought from the well were hardly adequate for the yearly job of scrubbing, cleaning, and making the house kosher. I always felt at that time what a pity it was that we couldn't bring out the beds themselves to be scrubbed. They could have used it. It was a marvelous bed. Like a drop-leaf table, the bed could be enlarged by pulling out a sliding board and thus allowed an almost unlimited number of people to sleep on it. Every couple of months the straw mattress was changed and a whole family could sleep there – and often did. In the room where the bed and table were, there was also a spare room and dressing room. During the day the bed was covered by a huge board and turned into a kitchen table. In a word, that was functional design.

I remember some special events that were engraved in my mind and now come back to my recollection. Suddenly I can envision the wedding of Joseph Bisberg. People from the whole town as well as the neighboring village of Nyesbizh were invited, and they all came. The whole wedding party rode proudly and brilliantly in horse-driven coaches provided by Aaron Bisberg, the father of the groom. We young girls presented floral bouquets to the bride. After the wedding all the guests, worn out from joy and celebrating, went to sleep in the barn that belonged to the bride's family. We never found out where the bride and groom spent the night.

And then there was the rare occasion when a carnival came to Strzegowo, with a merry-go-round, a magician, acrobats, and other talented performers. It was for us a world of miracle upon miracle.

But the greatest occasion of the year was when the geese-dealers came through the town with their flocks of snow-white, fat geese driven before them. While the whole town came out to watch this remarkable sight, the geese handlers used to keep their yearly rendezvous with Sarah-Vita to relish her wonderful specialties, in particular fish and egg noodles. And when the geese handlers had sated their appetites and left, disappearing over the horizon with their cackling flocks, like white clouds – that was when the celebrating just began because Sarah-Vita had prepared enough food not only for the dealers, but for the Novogrodsky clan and all the children of Strzegowo. What a holiday it was for us to eat that delicious fish and egg noodles! I can still taste all those delicacies.

There were also sad occasions as well. I remember when my father's whole stock of goods was stolen, and as a result he had to leave Strzegowo and his family and travel to America. How sad it was when just a year later our mother died and left seven orphans, ranging from six months to eleven years of age. One of my most vivid memories is of the night before our mother died, when Joseph Bisberg rode on horseback all night to a distant town, hoping to bring back a specialist to save her life. She was only thirty-two years old.

I remember very well how we left Strzegowo two years later. How moving it was to say farewell to our town. Aaron Bisberg cried and covered himself with tears as he put us in the wagon. I recall very clearly how this tall, powerful man stood in his doorway and wept like a small child at the thought of losing us. He loved us all so much and never lost the opportunity to show us the depth and sincerity of his affection.

This appears to be a saga of the Bisbergs, since their name appears so often. That's because we all felt that the Bisberg place was our second home. It was there that we were shown love, sheltered, and fed. To this day we can see that the Bisbergs, especially Feigl and Joe, even here in America, are maintaining the Bisberg tradition of helping others and standing in the forefront to provide leadership for the United Strzegowo Relief Committee, helping the survivors of the Holocaust wherever they may be.

RACHEL NOVOGRODSKY-STEINMAN

My Lost Ones

The Novogrodskys

My father, Aba, was born in Mlawa and came from a family of scholars. His brother, Faivl Novogrodsky, who lived in Strzegowo in his later years, was an accomplished person, a Torah scholar, an intelligent man. Everyone came to him for advice. But despite the fact that he was such an outstanding person, there was never a trace in his behavior of anything approaching conceit. He dealt with everyone warmly and on an equal basis. And at the same time, everyone in the town treated him with the greatest respect.

Faivl passed away in Strzegowo. The people of the town will never forget that master of the Talmud. May his memory be blessed.

Henekh, another brother, like Faivl was also a student of the Talmud and well versed as well in worldly affairs. He was also a scholar and a wonderful personality. He was quiet and modest and never raised his voice in anger; his reputation was legitimately earned. He lived half of his life in Mlawa and spent many years in Germany. Just before the coming of the Nazis to Germany, he was insulted for being Jewish, and determined to leave for Israel [then Palestine] where he also brought his family. After several years of living there, he passed away with honor and respect in his own land. We will always honor his memory.

Itsl Novogrodsky, the third brother, moved to Strzegowo shortly after his marriage and was very much like his brothers – a student of the Torah, a person with humane values, a man of distinction. But he was not able to make a good living in Strzegowo so he decided to leave for America in hopes of better luck. Even in America, Itsl's house was founded in Yiddishkait and piety. His house was always open to his compatriots and was a center of activities for people in New York's East Side. He died after a lengthy illness. We will also remember him with honor.

My father, Aba, was the youngest of the four brothers. He married a cousin named Malke Bzhoze from Warsaw, and shortly after the wedding he moved to Strzegowo. And as my father was a businessman, a hat maker, he was also one of the respected people in Strzegowo.

My father was quiet and refined in his business activities as well as his private life and received a great deal of respect and honor. He was very generous and always ready to provide help whenever the occasion demanded it. He never came back from the synagogue without a needy guest for the Sabbath. He lived his whole life in the spirit of the religious laws, which he carried out to the smallest detail. He prayed three times a day and in the evenings studied the holy scriptures. With deep feeling he thanked God for his ability to make a good living and allowing him to share his good fortune with others and study the Torah.

Despite his extreme piety, he was able to tolerate the Zionist movements [many of which were anti-orthodox] and even hoped one day to go to Israel [Palestine]. Unfortunately, that never came to pass and he met his death along with the other six million victims of our people, may their memory be blessed.

My Mother, Malkele

With deep sorrow, I recall the memory of my brilliant, loving, courteous, and pious mother. Quiet, gentle, tolerant, she always saw the bright side of things. Despite her extreme piety, she was also able to deal with worldly matters as well. In a quiet but determined way she took part in all the activities that were directed toward helping the sick and needy. She even founded one such organization herself. The whole town respected her for her deeply humane behavior. It's difficult for me to write about this. It's painful to recall how the barbarians took away her life.

You are with me in all the minutes and days of my life and my tears are your remembrance.

My Only Brother, Moyshe

My brother went to his death along with my parents. Young and sincere young man, blood of my blood, heart of my heart. How can I forget you? The whole town honored you for your honesty and sincerity. All the mothers in town were jealous of ours because of you. My dear brother, what wonderful children you would have had! How can I forget you? I will keep your memory until the last minute of my life.

Esther Leah Novogrodsky
Tel Aviv

From Israel

It was the winter of 1917. A cold wind is blowing and a heavy snow covers all. The window panes are covered with flowers of frost. We are standing near the heating stove to warm up a bit when suddenly the door of our house opens and our public school teacher, Nakhman Koren, comes in and turns gleefully to my brother – "Abramshe, Did you hear? We got Eretz Yisroel! We got the Balfour Declaration!" I was young then and I saw how the eyes of all those who heard him filled with tears of joy and I thought to myself, "We too shall have our own country."

We planned then to call for a general meeting in the synagogue. The news spread quickly throughout the town and all the members of the community took part in the celebration. The Zionists made the speeches. Abraham, my brother, embellished his speech with quotations from the Prophets and the Sages. The speech evoked opposition from the ultra-religious and the anti-Zionists, especially the Bund.

The Bund was flourishing at that time. Many of the town's intellectuals were Bundists. They had a large library at their disposal. The party organized evening classes and lectures concerning all aspects of socialism. Among the Bund leadership were Tamar Eidlitz, the Bisbergs, Goldbergs, Wilgolskys, Shapiras, and other families. One of their activities was to lay the foundation for a municipal library that later on was taken over by the Zionists.

People from Warsaw used to come to Strzegowo for vacation because of the clean air, the lovely countryside, and the campsite on the river just outside the town, which belonged to Itche Meir Piotrikowsky. The site was used for secret gatherings, for relaxation and fun and swimming in the river at the foot of the mountain.

Because the place belonged to a Jew, we were not afraid to be there. All kinds of political activities, illegal at the time, took place there. Children, of course, were not allowed to be there at such times, but who cared! We ran after them and took part in their courses, singing, and games. I remember how at that time we trembled as we sang "The Internationale." In years to come the campsite became a place for soccer, card games, etc. The Bund held its classes and lectures there because it was a convenient place, or out of fear of the Evil Eye or the parents and the authorities, who were all opposed to their movement. At that time, the Bund had a greater influence than the Mizrakhi [Zionist] party.

After the veteran members of the Bund went to America or other countries, new, young people appeared on the scene. At that time a Zionist organization, Tkhiya [rebirth], was founded. Among the founders were Moyshe Goldshlak, now living in the U.S., Malke Piotrikowsky, who is a Holocaust survivor and now lives in Israel, the sisters Ziskind, and others. They organized Zionist propaganda and Hebrew classes and took the place of the Bund. It did not take long for them to split up and disappear. But the seeds they sowed bore fruit some time later when the younger generation grew up.

The Zionist idea began to reverberate in the Beth-Hamidrash [the house of study] as well. The old people felt it and began to persecute the younger members of the study house. The young felt stifled, and they went out into the open and began to participate in all the Zionist activities. These boys founded the Hekhalutz-Hamizrakhi in Strzegowo. This was the beginning of open Zionist activity, with religion placed to the side.

I remember that in 1924, with the opening of the university in Jerusalem, the Hekhalutz-Hamizrakhi organized a public celebration with a procession bearing the Jewish flag. That was the first time that our town saw this sort of celebration. It culminated in the synagogue. It all made a great impression, and our new members joined the party. And yet the opposition of the older generation grew because they saw it all as "atheistic."

I should mention here the courage of those young people of

Hekhalutz-Hamizrakhi who went to the agricultural training farm in Shkotashkowa, near Rateshwintz. Members of Hekhalutz-Hamizrakhi were also active in the struggles during the election to the Polish parliament. They suffered a great deal because of the conflicts between fathers and sons. The news of the anti-Jewish riots in Palestine in 1929 shook up the people of the town. Life was not just celebrations. I will never forget the celebration and great joy in the town when Eliezer Gips and family went to Eretz Yisroel. Everyone came to see them off. Even the Poles who lived in the town, with the priest and nobility at the head. All the vehicles in the town were drafted for the occasion and covered with flowers and blue and white banners. Abraham Binem-Margolin, a man of intellect and education and an old-time Zionist, rode a white horse. He was later hanged by the Nazis, may his name be blessed. We danced in the streets together with our Polish neighbors. When Eliezer Gips parted from Hekhalutz-Hamizrakhi in the wood outside of town, he gave the secretary a symbolic coin, on condition that whoever is the first to go to Palestine should get it. As it happened this request was fulfilled when Shlomo Skavran was the next to go to Palestine.

I want to go back to the difficulties we had because of the political infighting with the town elders, in particular those who were teaching in the Beth-Midrash, because it was they who taught the Talmud and the commentaries. And there were also conflicts with the general Hekhalutz, which appeared on the scene with its slogans, attempting to attract people to their movement instead of Hekhalutz-Hamizrakhi. This of course created conflicts and ideological disputes between the two movements.

The various organizations called for special meetings during the holidays in order to raise money for the various charities. With all that has been said above, and all that was not mentioned here, it was not easy for those who wanted to instill a new spirit in the life of the town to penetrate the community. The town sent relatively large sums to the various funds. This too was not accomplished easily. We did it only by placing the "pushkes" [contribution boxes] in every household and having serious and dedicated people open them and collect the money. We also organized performances and parties in which all the members of the Zionist movement participated.

A general Zionist movement was also organized, cooperating with the youth of the town, because the various jealousies worked to awaken all those in the town who became indifferent. Those who heard all sorts of songs began to listen to new songs and new voices. From the old, who remembered times past, we often heard that we were destroying eternal life.

The Zionist organizations provided Saturday evening parties in which members of all the parties participated. It often happened that a lot of tension and strong discussions ensued concerning party issues. But as the saying goes, "Where authors vie, wisdom increases." Even the left and right Poalei Zion were organized properly and their activities were praiseworthy. Just as among all Talmud scholars, so also in Strzegowo, we had an organization called "The Daily Page Scholars." Even though most of them belonged to the Hapoel-Hamizrakhi and so strong ties were created with all those who held the Torah dear, they too took an active part in all the Zionist activities and it is thanks to these organizations that some of them remained alive and are now living in Israel.

"The end of man is to die. And no one can alter the past." But who was it that allowed the cruel Nazi hand to uproot and destroy the lives of those whose presence will remain in our memory and the memory of the generations to come?

May these lines honor the Jewish community of Strzegowo, which was destroyed, and may they serve in place of a monument to their memory since no place remains on which to erect it. Only the heavens can cover their ashes; and we will carry their memory in our hearts together with our wrath and eternal curses on the Nazis, a curse that will follow them until they all perish.

YITZKHAK TANDITSHARZEN
Translated from Hebrew by Tamar Rawitz

And if Your Child Asks, "What Is That . . . ?"

Dear Children! You may be surprised sometimes at the strange fact that your parents are often drawn to one book on their bookshelf, the language of which you may not even understand. But precisely this book is so dear to them, creates a tumult in their hearts, and makes tears well in their eyes. The following is meant to explain the reason for this and your connection with the content of this "book of tears."

Poland was a land in which there was one of the largest and most significant concentrations of Jews – many hundreds of communities, in each of which flourished all phases of community life: Torah study, as well as scientific and literary inquiry. One of these was our ancestral home, Strzegowo.

Polish Jewry nourished all Jewish communities throughout the Diaspora with its spiritual richness. Polish Jewry managed to maintain its spiritual independence in spite of all the trials and tribulations visited upon it by its neighboring peoples. It may truly be said of Polish Jewry that the greater its trial, the more it flourished. The saying goes, "When you are persecuted, increase and multiply." And also, the more troubles they faced, the more there was of mutual help and responsibility.

After Russian Jewry lost its vitality, it was Polish Jewry, with all its educational and cultural institutions, social help, hundreds of Yeshivas, schools, high schools, writers, rabbis, and public figures, that became the greatest and strongest reservoir of Zionist activity. That is where your parents were raised, educated, and learned and absorbed Yiddishkait and Zionism. That is where your roots are.

Our town, Strzegowo, was situated on the road from Mlawa to Plotzk, which went on toward central Prussia. It was a rather new town, and yet it absorbed all the best of Polish-Jewish culture. Although it did not have a tradition rooted in the past, its fresh, young spirit provided a certain charm.

Its Jewish population was small, but just as in large communities there were houses of prayer, schools, public institutions, libraries, and political parties. All this was accomplished during the brief span of its existence.

It brought up a young generation that was proud of its accomplishments. They were taught ideals, pioneering, and the values of all the workers' movements that were active at the time, including the Bund, Poale-Zion, and others. Some went on to realize their ideals in the U.S. and other parts of the world, some in Eretz-Yisroel.

But to our terrible and great sorrow, the wrath of the Nazi oppressors was wrought upon the greatest part of the Jews of Strzegowo as well as the rest of Polish Jewry. Like all the other Jewish communities, the Jews of Strzegowo were deported to death camps where they were cruelly tortured and killed. And this was done by a nation that prided itself as the bearers of the height of civilization but actually perpetrated the depths of baseness and wickedness.

Dear children! In this book you will find the story of the Jewish community in Strzegowo, from its beginnings until its tragic end. You will be able to read about the Jews who lived there, including your grandmothers and grandfathers and all their relatives, about their lives and their dreams that were never realized.

Most of this book was written in Yiddish, the language in which your fathers and forefathers spoke and breathed, and which filled their lives. This is why you should become familiar with the content of this book, and your parents will certainly be interested in explaining whatever you don't understand in the original. This Yizkor book was published in the U.S. by those of our town who live there, and thus it serves as an eternal memorial to the pure saints who perished there.

This will have accomplished the following: that all this will not be forgotten for generations to come, that you will absorb into your bloodstream what the Nazi Amalek, the heinous criminals, have done to us, and so that you should remember those that never lived to fulfill their wishes and their plans. Thus we will see some consolation.

JOSEPH ROSENBERG
Translated from Hebrew by Tamar Rawitz

Before the War and the Beginning of the Martyrdom of Strzegowo

I am one of those who lived through the first experiences of the Jews of Strzegowo. I am one of the very few who can look at the results of the fatality and with a wave of my hand say: "What can we do? We have our great God in the heavens. What he will decide to do with the people of Israel, will indeed be done."

Every personal initiative died off. As a result a great many young people like myself and many others decided to leave their homes in order to save themselves from a catastrophe. They failed to have the logical idea to cross the borders and pay attention to the real goal – to escape to Israel.

In order to better understand the circumstances that took place before the outbreak of the war, I'll go back and attempt to describe some occurrences in the last days before the outbreak of the war. The Polish radio in the time before the beginning of the war poisoned the air with rumors that the Germans will not triumph against Poland or France or England because their tanks are ersatz, and every bullet can go right through them. As a consequence, no one fully understood the bestiality of Hitler's legions.

The whole summer of 1939 was full of military activities. Polish units on their way to the German border used to stop in Strzegowo. So the actual outbreak of the war did not surprise anyone. Friday, the day the war broke out, was a day like all the Fridays of the year. Housewives baked *khales* and cooked fish for the Sabbath. We were just Jews, so why should we disturb our sense of the coming Sabbath?

But the next morning we suddenly had a sense of what war would be. We could hear the sounds of canons from Mlawa, and Strzegowo quickly filled with refugees who had fled from Mlawa and neighboring towns and were beginning to tell the gruesome stories of war: how people were torn out of their homes by bombs; how mothers pined for their children and whole families were lost. A horror had overtaken the people.

And suddenly there emerged the stupid anti-Semite Mtuvshevski, who became a big shot. He lived near Khaim Fatog, against whom he held a strong hatred. He used his power to control him and forced him to work on that very Sabbath. When Khaim complained, Mtuvshevski called in gendarmes and forced him to work. People were forced to dig trenches. By Sunday, the Nazi beasts had come to Strzegowo and the rumor that the Germans will not stand was totally discredited. All day German planes flew undisturbed, and clearly the lies of the Polish radio were exposed. Around three o'clock in the afternoon a new squadron of German airplanes arrived and bombed the town of Strzegowo.

The terror that released is undescribable. People ran like crazed animals looking for shelter. And how grotesque it was as people went running for shelter, seeking shelter in wooden houses and even in such places as behind a door or under a bed or in other such places that offered no real protection. The hysterical shrieks of the women – "Hear O Israel!"– was mixed with the frightened yells of children.

The bombardment continued without stop for half an hour, and thereafter a grizzly portrait of the town could be seen. Houses were torn up, and there was no one to put out the many fires. Toward the outskirts of town many houses were burned, and many people also were killed from the flames. It came to pass that the whole town packed up and began to run in the direction of Plinsk through many roads and even alleys, in small wagons or on foot. With others of our neighbors we prepared to leave but were held up by the advice of Israel Rosen, who counseled that if a bomb exploded three meters away and no one was wounded, then we should stay where we were.

But shortly thereafter the houses began burning, and we decided we should try to escape. But it happened that a wagon driver had left a small horse behind. It was dark and we couldn't see him very well, but we packed on the wagon all our food, clothing, and bedding, and the women on top, and we began to make our way. However, it was only after we were out of town that we could see the fearful victims. All around us there was fire. But after having traveled several kilometers, our horse stopped and wouldn't go any further. After we rearranged some of the stuff in the wagon and gave him a push, he went on for another couple of kilometers and then stopped again. This time nothing helped. He spread his legs and gave up the ghost.

We remained unmoving in the middle of the night, lost and bewildered. None of the passersby were willing to stop for a group of beggars. Finally someone who was traveling by with two healthy horses agreed to pick us up for a little money and we were once more on our way. But when dawn came we found ourselves surrounded on every side. Peasants with all their goods, cows, pigs, chickens, and with their wives and children, some on foot and some riding were all around us and we couldn't move from the spot. And the airplanes appeared again and began bombing the road. The people dispersed and ran into the fields. Many of the wagons and horses were torn apart and the horses killed. This all happened as if in one flash of the eye. We didn't see the horses any longer, so we carried a few things on our shoulders and started off again in the direction of Plinsk and were bombed again. By this time it hardly made any impression on us, and with some other families we took refuge in an abandoned house that used to belong to a rich man.

I'm not able to describe the circumstances and adventures in Plinsk because that's a large and separate story in itself. But here we had our first experiences with the Nazi beasts and were able to see what fate awaited us. Like robbers with wild cries they forced themselves into the town, and their first "heroic" act was to empty into the streets all the goods and fruits of the marketplace; they went into the best stores and took everything without paying. They said they had an account that they would repay in time . . .

After a short time among strangers we returned to Strzegowo. The town looked like a cemetery. Still and without activity we hoped that someone would appear in the streets. Slowly and sadly people began to return, each with their own bag of woes. In what they had lived through, everyone had the same question – what will happen next?

And here I'd like to recount an episode that someone told me about, which happened in Strzegowo while I was absent. When the Germans marched into Strzegowo the streets were empty. But they spotted a man standing near his house, with his hands in his pockets, a cigarette between his lips and his mustache turned up. So they took him for an Aryan and bestowed all honors on him. They were astounded when he declared himself to be a Jew. That was Leibl the baker. Surely he was not someone to be envied. In that time there was barely a *minyan* of Jews left.

The Germans then began to show all their ugliness. When they discovered that there were a great many food products hidden in the cellar of David Tikn they confiscated everything, threw Tikn and his family out and occupied the house themselves. The same happened with Piotrikowsky's mill which they captured. The accountant, who was my sister, was also detained so they could become familiar with all the businesses in town. It's easy to imagine how my sister felt in such an atmosphere. During the time that my sister worked with the mill, she was concerned to provide her customers with the best products, as much as anyone needed. But that did not last for very long. A representative for the Germans soon appeared and saw my sister in her office and snarled, "What are the filthy Jews doing here?" They sent her away immediately and totally took over the mill.

Around that time the first phase of the crazed Nazis ended – our "good times" compared with what was to come. Up until that time – around four weeks – we suffered. But then the second phase began. They began to cover the whole community. They began insulting and delivering pain to all of us. Every day the Nazis needed to fulfill a quota of people for slave labor. Now every Jew experienced moments of the deepest torment and pain, not only because of the pain of working in the market but also because of the unending insults. Anti-Semitic Poles together with the Nazis vied with each other in outstanding laughter to see how the Jews swept up the streets or did other demeaning work. At the same time they played games, throwing rocks at the Jews and trying to strike them in the head. From time to time a Nazi would run over to a Jew with his rifle or revolver at the ready and say, "Jew, I'm going to shoot you" and laugh wildly. That was in order to terrify the Jew and those around him.

It makes me think of a final episode that I'll never forget. The Nazi leader suddenly decided to attack us once again. So he yelled, "The Jews are nothing!" The Jews quickly got together and began to sing "Hatikvah," and the singing was strong and fiery. All of them sang together the anthem of Zionism.

Since this obviously made a great impression on the Nazis, their leader inquired what the meaning of the song was. "Hope," was our answer. Hope, he stated, and burst out laughing, and foaming at the mouth yelled out, "What? You shitty Jews still have hope? Even now at this time?"

We felt at that time so low, as if someone had stepped on us. We felt so insulted at that moment of ecstasy and holiness. This had a great impact on me, and I felt it was crazy to stay here under the insults and pain affecting our national honor. Anyone with a drop of humanity left must leave. And the time was with us. There were stories that the Russian Army was already in Pultusk and would be in Strzegowo tomorrow. With trembling hearts people waited to be rescued. I took advantage of the moment to run across the border. There were only five of us who left together.

It was in the month of November when I left our little town. It was hard to say farewell to Strzegowo where I experienced so much pain but also so much joy. Above all it was hard to leave the family in such a difficult position. I squelched it all and felt only the good fortune of my life. And so I am one of the few fortunate ones who remained alive.

ISRAEL SILBERSTROM
Israel, 1951

The Strzegowo Ghetto

The Way It Began

Preface

A terrifying shudder pervades my body, my blood and veins seem frozen as I write and think about those sorrowful and difficult wartime years and relive them in my mind. I can see again the people who were so dear and close to me. They were those with whom I studied and worked, and who I hoped would survive to tell this story with joy.

Unhappily, none of them is alive anymore. They were all, in atrociously savage circumstances, put to death. They have all disappeared with the wind, all have been taken under by darkness, and I alone have escaped to tell you.[7]

Of the whole Jewish community that lived in Strzegowo during the wartime years, only three survived: two young boys [Yoblanski and Fabian] and I. There were also a few who had escaped early from Strzegowo, some to the Soviet Union. Everything was destroyed and annihilated. There are no words with which to describe the frightful and tragic events. We had an expression, when troubles enveloped everyone and no one was spared: there is no house without a corpse. Today, unfortunately, we need to say: there is no house with a living person. Of hundreds of families who lived there, not one has remained alive. It's hard to think about and even harder to write about it.

But we must steel ourselves in order to discuss the specific conditions of life in the Strzegowo ghetto.

7. Bogen gives this first in Hebrew and then in Yiddish, paraphrasing the lines from the Book of Job, in which Job is told about the destruction of his family and possessions.

It would not be right on my part if I should report only the "better" conditions of the Strzegowo ghetto without reporting on the devotion and self-sacrifices of the leaders of that era. Not only the leaders brought about the positive results we achieved, but the whole Jewish community played its part in the circumstances. Every individual in the town contributed what he was able to do under the most severe discipline and with the highest sense of responsibility. We can clearly say and underscore the fact that during the whole time there was not one occasion when one person exercised power over another. Anyone who knows the history of life in the ghettos will appreciate the fact that in Strzegowo there was not one act of denunciation or slander. Such was the honor of the Strzegowo community.

And to you, my former fellow participants in that tragic time, forgive me for paying so little attention to your worthy actions and self-sacrifices while trying to do justice to the contributions of the community at large. Since I was often personally involved with your heroic activities, I often understated the praise that was deserving. One more thing needs to be added here: since there have been many outcries against so-called *Judenräte*, I take it to be my duty to declare openly that everything that was done in Strzegowo during the course of the terrible war years occurred with my consent and personal responsibility. I take pride in it and thank God that I was worthy to be involved there.

Friday, 1 September 1939, four o'clock in the morning of that historically significant day. The morning stars still twinkled, the first rays of the sun slowly began to cut through the dawn's darkness.

The deep sleep of the little town of Strzegowo was suddenly interrupted. One could hear in the distance some strange sounds and detonations. Here and there shutters are hurriedly opened, windows open and people peer out with fearful looks. Clusters of people begin to assemble, half-clothed and overwrought. On everyone's face you can read the fear that comes from not knowing the meaning of the reports that could be heard in the distance.

Everyone seeks an answer, an explanation. Some said: "Those are just probably the sounds of thunder, and we're hearing the echo from afar." "How is that possible?" others retorted. "The skies are clear, there isn't a sign of clouds, the horizon is clear and bright. There can't be the echo of thunder." But as if to reassure themselves in order to convince others, it was argued that it was just military exercises. That's how people tried to talk themselves into believing anything except what was represented by the terrible word: war.

The sound of explosions from afar become ever louder and closer, and the anxiety among the people grows from minute to minute. While people were still standing around discussing the meaning of the clangor, the first auto arrived, carrying refugees from Mlawa, who were witnesses to the fact that war had broken out and that Mlawa had already been bombed by the Luftwaffe and heavy artillery.

The first victim in Mlawa was a Jewish man named Silverberg. This was a sinister omen signifying that in this frightful war, Jews would suffer the most.

It's easy to imagine the panic that overtook the whole town. Although it was Friday, when Jewish housewives were usually totally involved in preparing for the Sabbath, this time everything was forgotten. People just stood around wringing their hands and breathing deep sighs from the depths of their hearts.

The turmoil continued to grow. Every car that arrived with refugees from Mlawa and neighboring towns served to increase the panic. There were some optimists who calmed people down and explained that in every unexpected circumstance there are always those panic-mongers and fear-mongers who are not satisfied until all their concerns are transferred to the crowds surrounding them. In fact, they maintained, there is nothing to really be afraid of. The Polish army is strong enough to break through the German lines so that the battle will be played out on German territory.

Those who attempted thus to calm people down were clearly just trying to convince themselves that nothing was wrong. The old expression, "We won't even lose a button," was one hundred percent right. The proof is that only a small number of cars with refugees from Mlawa had arrived.

For a moment the crowds calmed down. The women began to go about their work. "After all," they said, "it's still the time to prepare for the Sabbath." The men, both Jews and Gentiles, began to carry out the orders of the local military forces, which had in the meantime taken over from the provincial town authorities and given various directives, among them an order to dig trenches against bombing. We all quickly set about digging the trenches, not realizing how ineffective they would be against air attacks.

Friday after lunch the panic increased. The refugees from Mlawa came in ever-increasing numbers. It became necessary to deal with the great numbers of people, to provide housing, and at least to furnish minimum necessities.

Spontaneously, as if self-generated, there developed a help committee consisting of the following people: Shmuel Berish Rosenberg and David Sokolow [Faivil Novogrodsky's son-in-law], who immediately began to work energetically to provide housing and take care of the other needs of the Mlawa refugees. I should add that it was unnecessary for us to invoke any kind of agitation or propaganda techniques. In keeping with its usual enlightened attitude, the people of Strzegowo this time also brought to bear their willingness to provide whatever each one could contribute to the demands of the situation. Every door was opened to take care of the people to the fullest extent that was possible. When all the private housing was filled, others were housed in the synagogue and some outlying structures in the town. We also provided food and drink and other basic necessities. We all believed naively that in these first several difficult weeks we would remain secure in the town.

This false illusion was quickly shattered on Sunday around three o'clock. A squadron of twenty-six bomber planes suddenly attacked Strzegowo. They came in low and without hindrance over the helpless town, dropping their heavy bombs and spraying the area with their machine guns. It's hard to understand, even to this day, how the town was not totally annihilated at that time. A great many people were killed, mostly Gentiles but also a few Jews, including some of the Mlawa refugees.

Everything was burning around the town and the destruction became greater and greater. Men, women, and children abandoned everything and began moving on the roads to Plonsk. Since there was no transportation available, everyone went on foot. The cries of the children echoed to the skies. The numbers of those escaping grew larger and larger. Also the peasants from nearby areas added to the stream of refugees. And all ran, urged on by the terrible portent – whereto?

Several days later the German army marched through Strzegowo and beyond. In the town there was a funereal calm. Slowly the people began turning back to their homes. The local authorities were replaced by the resident ethnic Germans. It was now clearly a question of war.

Although at the outset there were no Reich Nazis in the town, there was still great fear. All the shops were closed. As much as possible, people didn't venture forth into the streets. They were simply afraid to stick their heads out of the doorways of their houses. At the same time, the ethnic Germans began to feel their power and started stealing, first from the stores and then the possessions in the houses, including furniture, clothing, and other materials.

The Jews had to report every morning to the open market, and there they were assigned to various tasks. One group was sent to repair the highways, which had been destroyed by the heavy artillery. The others were distributed among the ethnic Germans and ordered to carry out whatever tasks they were commanded to perform. As it appeared to us, a slave market was set up, except that in a slave market there was some remuneration while here there was none. The services were free, gratis. In the Jewish community people all held the same view. All commercial activity was strictly forbidden. People were also prevented from gathering together and in the evenings everyone had to be in their own homes. It was even forbidden to visit a neighbor who lived in the same dwelling. The regulations were closely enforced to be sure the people were obeying them. And woe to those who were caught breaking any of the rules . . .

On one occasion there was a meeting of the library committee, consisting of several people and myself as chair. We decided that we needed to save the great treasure of our library, which consisted of thousands of extremely valuable books. So we packed all the books in boxes, and on a dark, rainy night, when we thought that the night watch was staying indoors to protect themselves from the rain, we slipped out and brought all the books to the Jewish cemetery. After we buried all the books, we were afraid that we might be stopped on the way back and questioned about our activities. So we spent the whole night in the cemetery and waited until morning when we returned one by one to our homes.

About two months later the first units of the German military police arrived. In the house where the local police used to be housed, all the windows had been blown out by the first bombing raid. So the Germans sent for a glazier to restore all the windows and put the place in order. At that time the only Jewish glazier in Strzegowo, Barukh Rebek [known as "Small-change Barukh"], terrified as he was, set to work repairing the damage. When he was done installing all the windows, the leader of the German police acknowledged that he had done a good job. Then he declared that from then on Barukh had to arrive every morning at six o'clock to light the stoves for the house and polish all the boots of the military police. With a heavy heart and a feigned smile on his face, Barukh said, "Jawohl, *Herr Post Leader*," and immediately set about his new responsibilities.

Exile

In many neighboring towns the separation of the Jews had already begun. In Froshnits and Astrolanka, all the Jews had been sent to the Russian side. In Ratshoynu and Sherpts, during a terrible scene, the Jews were sent to Warsaw. In Rupin and neighboring towns the expulsion decree had taken in all the people, and many on their own started filling the road to Warsaw. There were no means of transportation, and in any case the bridge in the direction of Modlin was still destroyed. The use of autos by civilians was forbidden so the only form of transportation left was by horse and wagon. Every family that could, bought a horse and wagon and packed all their goods and belongings and started on their way.

Understandably, on the way people would stop off in the towns to feed and water the horses and to slip into a house for a while to warm their bones, which were frozen by the cold. Some people stopped in the devastated towns, and the great majority of wanderers stopped in Mlawa, Strzegowo, and Plonsk. The fear of the exile notices also fell on Strzegowo, so some of the people started out for Warsaw. Suddenly there was a rumor that the entire population of Jews in Mlawa faced an exile edict. It's easy to imagine the panic that seized everyone. People began packing feverishly despite the fact that it was forbidden to take anything along. One wore as many clothes as possible and lay down to sleep, waiting for the dreadful edict to be enforced.

Around that time, in January of 1940, Strzegowo was appointed the central headquarters for the surrounding area, except for Mlawa. As a result a whole new complement of German soldiers arrived, with a lieutenant colonel at the head. You can imagine the fear and horror that overtook the Jewish community in the town. The arrival of so many military police seemed a sign of bad things to come. Others saw the concentration of police as a clear indication that an expulsion order for the Jews was soon to come. Everyone became convinced that such things would inevitably occur.

Among the community leaders the idea was developed that a Jewish delegation should go to the leader of the gendarmes in order to make a connection with the source to see what the basic situation was. Among the people available at that time – Yekhiel Nathan Burstein, Eliezer Gips, David Tik, Israel Rosen, Shmuel Dov Rosenberg, Yekhiel Piotrikowsky, David Sokolow, and Moyshe Mikhel Saperstein – no one was willing to take the risk to go into the lion's den. It was then decided that the responsibility should fall on the rabbi, Jacob Solomon Simyatitsky, the logical spokesperson for the community. Under the pressure of the circumstances, the rabbi agreed but with the condition that I should accompany him to the meeting. It was not easy for me to accept the assignment, but with the urging of Shmuel Rosenberg and Israel Rosen, I agreed.

Since Barukh Rebek was working in the headquarters in charge of lighting the stoves and polishing boots, we asked him to tell the leader of the gendarmes that a delegation from the Jewish community would like to meet with him; if he was willing, we asked him to set the time and place for the meeting. Barukh brought us the positive decision – we should meet him at eleven in the morning at his headquarters.

When we arrived at the appointed hour, we saw before us a tall, broad-boned man who looked us over from head to toe. The rabbi instantly began to shake, broke out in a cold sweat and was incapable of uttering a word. The lieutenant colonel addressed himself to the rabbi: "*Bitte*, have a seat, Herr rabbi," he said and pushed a chair in his direction. That action had the effect of relieving my own fearfulness, and I immediately took the initiative to explain the basis of our visit. He first made clear his positions, which had to do with the future of the Jews.

He then developed the following positions: there is no question that the Germans do not foresee the possibility of Jews living among them in the town. Their separation from the area is a virtual certainty. But it is his view that the expulsion should not be carried out in the midst of the ferocious winter, people being sent out barefoot and naked, as was done in many neighboring towns. He then proposed that we make a complete census of the Jews in Strzegowo, deliver the list to him and begin to make our own plans for the exodus to Warsaw. Among the first to leave should be the most wealthy people, who have enough money to find suitable places even in the winter time. Then those with less money should be the next to go until finally the town should be cleansed of Jews. He then explained that he would give us four months, that is until May, to make Strzegowo "Judenrein." We were to organize a help committee to collect money from the rich and to help out the poorer citizens of the town. Every month he asked us to provide a report to indicate how many and who were the people who have left and what the status of the relief committee was. If we agree and carry out his orders, he assures us that as long as he is in charge in Strzegowo, nothing bad will happen to the Jews. He made me personally responsible for carrying out his edicts.

When the people saw us return from the meeting safely, they almost danced with joy. We repeated word for word what we had been told by the lieutenant colonel, and, as usual, there developed immediately a debate about what he really meant. We tried to find in his words a trick to deceive us because we could simply not imagine that a person in his position, a German and a Nazi, should be trying in any way to lighten the burden placed upon us. We finally concluded that we had no real choices in the matter. We would simply have to wait and see what would happen in time.

Accordingly, we organized the relief committee, which consisted of Eliezer Gips, David Sokolow, Anshel Stavitsky, Barukh Rebek, Shmuel Ber Rosenberg, Fishl Klapman, and myself. We collected money every week and distributed it to the poorer members of the community. We also made a census of all the Jews, which consisted at that time of 565 souls. Very few people left the town then. The rabbi was an exception. He was terribly frightened by our first encounter with the German officer and left as soon as he could.

In Warsaw at that time there was a dreadful epidemic of typhus. Sanitary conditions were terrible, and there was a shortage of food, so the people of Strzegowo decided to try and stay where they were as long as possible. I have to confess that the attitude of the Germans toward the people in Strzegowo was responsible. We got to know them better and better, and that enabled us to lead a relatively normal life. Since I knew the lieutenant colonel quite well, he told me confidentially that until Hitler and the Nazis came to power, he had been a member of the German Communist Party and fought actively against Hitlerism. I believe that he was telling the truth and his general attitude towards the Jews seemed to substantiate his statements. And also, by that time he had relaxed many of his edicts that had been directed toward us. We began to organize ourselves and began to bribe them in various ways; they actually took money from us for concessions. That had a terrific impact. In that way we could effect everything from the smallest requests to some significant changes, and we were able to bring about over time a lightening of the pressures on us.

In the beginning of the summer of 1940 the municipal government, which had been under the direction of the ethnic Germans and was brutal in its attitude toward the Jews, was replaced by regular German S. A. forces. There was an instant sense of foreboding. The new group marched through the town proudly in their brown shirts, and our hearts trembled at the thought of this new group with their new orders and requirements. But we also began to think of ways to deal with the new group as well.

We still at that time had to deal with the order for all Jews to assemble in the morning in one particular place. The ethnic Germans then chose people to work for them, as many as they pleased. They provided no remuneration for the work and used people in a brutal manner.

The worst was on the Sabbath. They ordered that the main square and the streets should be made spotlessly clean. It was their order that this task should be carried out by the most orthodox Jews in the town. It's hard to describe the pain and the heartbreak engendered by that terrible scene in which the most pious Jews, such as Yitzkhak Friedman, Israel Rosen, Moyshe the Shoykhet, Shmuel Berish Rosenberg, Beryl Klapman, and others stood all day on the Sabbath with brooms in their hands, cleaning the streets. On the basis of our arrangements with the lieutenant colonel, we determined immediately to establish relationships with the new Nazi civil government and to explain the tragic conditions under which we lived. We were lucky also this time to encounter an individual who indicated a willingness to work with us. According to his orders, there was established a new committee to represent the Jewish community, consisting of Barukh Rebek as liaison with the new German group, Yudel Stavitsky as chair of the labor Zionist group,

Moyshe Mikhel Saperstein representing the orthodox circle, and myself for the Zionist group.

With the agreement of the police and the high commissioner, we came to the following agreements:

1. Jews who are chosen to work will be remunerated.
2. The Jews will no longer have to assemble every day on the market place. The community will decide on its own by turns who will be required to appear.
3. It is not always necessary for a particular person to do the work. When necessary another can be substituted.
4. Several people over the age of sixty were relieved of work assignments.
5. One person who will be paid by the community will be in charge of cleaning the market place and the streets, so the tragic image of the orthodox so engaged will no longer be seen. He arranged to do the work on Friday afternoons.

The foregoing points were for us a great accomplishment. The number of people forced to labor decreased because it was now necessary for them to be paid. Also we were able to organize the responsibilities so everyone knew when his turn was coming. Also there were a number of people who willingly volunteered for the work assignments and also gladly agreed to substitute for others.

The Jewish community lifted its spirits a bit and gradually began to order its life and with spirit and money lightened the burden of its condition.

There even began to develop a significant commerce with manufactured articles. Some manufacturers from Lodz sent us goods, which we were able to smuggle to Mlawa and Plonsk and sell quite a few to Gentiles in these towns. In that way a good number of people in the town were able to support themselves. Others were able to work with handicrafts and other small activities so that although we had shortened rations, compared with the situations of other towns, we never suffered from hunger. And at the same time we were able to get almost all that we wanted. The general business climate gradually came to something almost approaching normal. We also dug up the books we had previously buried in the grave-yard, and since they were in good condition we distributed them among the young people who exchanged them among themselves.

The Beginning of the End

In 1941 the Nazis began to develop their devilish plans to extermi-nate the Jewish people. The first part of the plan was to concentrate the people in special locations. From what they called their "pro-tectorate," they began exporting Jews to Warsaw, where there al-ready were more than half a million people. Hunger and terrible epidemics raged there and increased in virulence from day to day. There also developed the fear that we too faced a similar fate. We could see that it had been established as a principle that Jews needed to be concentrated in ghettos. In order to prevent ourselves from being exported to Warsaw, we decided to establish a ghetto in Strzegowo and to carry out the plan we decided upon the follow-ing: we contacted the head of the medical unit, and for the price of a luxury automobile that we would provide him, we would fabri-cate a typhus epidemic in the town. We took several people to the hospital and injected them so they would show a high fever. Then we invited the head of the medical unit to inspect them. He then sent a report to the high circles of the Nazi organization and explained that the entire Jewish population needed to be quaran-tined in order to prevent the disease from spreading to the rest of the community. We pursued this plan and the order soon came to organize a ghetto on the spot for the entire community.

The order came on Sukkoth 1941 and decreed that all the Jews should within forty-eight hours be sequestered in the ghetto, whose boundaries were located near the area where the pig market used to be. Although we had planned for the ghetto to be estab-lished, fulfilling the move in such a short time was very difficult. It was not possible to place every family in a separate building. We had to put two or three families in a structure. And the problem of how to determine where the people would be comfortable was hard to figure out. But everyone was very cooperative, and by the appointed time the entire community had accomplished the move with all their effects. By the end of Sukkoth, the young people had worked intensively to set up the walls and to enclose the ghetto. There was one door for entry and exit, and by Simkhas Torah we had succeeded in isolating ourselves totally from the outside world, locked in among ourselves.

It was a sorrowful gathering together, and there was an air of sadness, a remembrance of Tisha b'Av in the midst of Simkhas Torah.[8]

But we needed to pull ourselves together and put things in order to get accustomed to our new situation. It was determined to organize a committee to deal with the new requirements that obtained in the ghetto. The committee was also charged with keeping up contacts with the outside world. Our physical and material conditions were not significantly changed. The local authorities did not alter their approach to us, and thus we hoped and prayed to be able to survive the war.

A few months later there was once again a resolution that all the smaller Jewish communities must be liquidated. There began a new series of movements and lobbying of the local authorities with the aim of establishing one large concentration of Jews in Mlawa. Eliezer Perlmutter, the leader of the Mlawa ghetto, and I were able to bribe the local authorities with ten thousand marks, two valuable rugs, and a caracul fur coat for one of the officials' wives. The plan was to create a large ghetto in Mlawa that would encompass Strzegowo and several of the neighboring towns. Perlmutter was determined to be the organizer of this movement. The authorities added one more street to the existing ghetto in Mlawa by evacuating the Gentiles who lived there, and the expulsions began immediately. The first to move were the Jews from Shransk, Rodzhanova, and Zhalin. Then a new problem arose. There was no room left in Mlawa for Strzegowo Jews. We numbered then about seven hun-

8. Tisha b'Av is the day on which the destruction of both temples is recalled and lamented.

dred souls, and as there were no more homes available in the Gentile community, we seemed doomed to be sent to Warsaw. Once more we bribed the local authorities to create a larger ghetto in Strzegowo that would also contain the Jews from Sherpts and Bezoyn, who also had been ordered to Warsaw.

On 6 January 1942 military vehicles brought to the doors of our ghetto more than a thousand people from those towns, carrying with them their small bundles.

It's hard to describe the condition of those poor, terrified, and beaten and bloodied people who seemed to be on their last legs. The Strzegowo help committee ran out and under a hail of blows on their shoulders from the SS helped the people into the safety of the ghetto as soon as possible. The SS didn't dare follow the people into the ghetto for fear of contracting some disease, which we had earlier convinced them was raging among the Jews.

Here the Jews of Strzegowo expressed so humane and caring a concern for the people that it's hard to paint in words. By the time night came, all the newcomers had been given lodging. A community kitchen was set up that served four hundred lunches every day. The overcrowding was incredible, with more than ten people to a room. This was undertaken with the knowledge that a humanitarian effort of the first rank was being implemented.

The End

In February 1942 the Nazis began to execute the final solution for the few remaining Jews in the area. About two hundred people who somehow survived heard about the ghetto in Strzegowo and managed to get to us, and we took them in as well.

All the Jewish ghettos at that time underwent horrible experiences. The Nazis attempted to drive the Jews into a fearful state of depression and to deprive them of the will to survive, so in each ghetto they undertook new acts of terror: this included the shooting or hanging of inmates in full view of the other people in the ghetto. In our area the first victims were the members of the local committees. In Mlawa, for example, they shot Perlmutter and hanged four others. Several days later they hanged fifteen people, all leaders of the various relief committees. Then a little later, even more savagely, they shot another fifty people.

We got the news from Mlawa that on 20 April our ghetto would be dismantled by the local gendarmes. We knew how that would go. Everyone was informed and warned to put together all their necessary effects, clothing, food, and any valuable objects. It was decided that the people would leave the ghetto the next morning.

At around seven in the morning the ghetto was attacked by the police units, one of which with its leader went about beating up everyone they could lay their hands on. When they discovered that the leaders had escaped, they threatened to kill everyone if the leaders didn't give themselves up. The demand was given to us and it created a real dilemma. Very few people were willing to return to a certain death. Early the next morning I retraced my steps and entered the door of the ghetto again.

Among the other members of the leadership, Barukh Rebek was hidden by some Poles in a nearby town. But he was soon found and shot by the local German police. Some others managed to escape to the Plonsk ghetto where they remained until that one was liquidated.

From the moment that I returned I was greeted with such a beating that I can't imagine to this day how I survived. I was immediately arrested and sent to Mlawa. I was imprisoned in a cellar underneath the office of the police, my arms chained behind my back, chains around my neck attached to the wall, and my right foot also chained to the wall. In that condition I remained for forty-eight days, during which I never had a drop of water for washing myself or shaving. I looked like a wild and demented person. Every once in a while I was taken upstairs to be interrogated. Each time anew I dreaded what the pain and torture would be. Beatings were the least of it. They even stuck hot wires under my nails – and worse.

They were mainly interested in discovering how we managed to keep the ghetto in such good shape. According to the meager rations we were given, they estimated that half of the people should have died, but the outcome was different from what they expected. There was not only no death, we lived and looked like normal people. They knew of course that we had help from Poles and even from Germans, and what they wanted was the precise information on who helped and how it was carried out.

All the attempts from various sources to obtain my freedom were unsuccessful. The chief who arrested me and led the interrogations was hoping to get a special recognition if he were able to force me to talk. The promotion in rank he hoped to obtain was more important to him than the bribes of money and jewelry that were offered to him.

One day on a Friday afternoon I was brought upstairs to the office. After the routine beating the chief started asking me questions:

"Have you ever heard the story of the burning of the Reichstag?"

"Jawohl."

"Do you know why the perpetrator confessed?"

"Nein."

"I'll explain it to you. He received a special injection of a truth serum and so he told everything he knew."

Then he continued. "Did you know that in 1936 there were a series of political trials in Moscow?"

"Jawohl."

"And did you know that all the conspirators confessed?"

"Jawohl."

"Do you know why?"

"Nein."

"Then let me explain. They were injected with a truth serum and told all. The same thing will happen to you tomorrow. You will be injected with the truth serum and will tell us everything we want to know."

Then they returned me to the cellar and left me there by myself. I was covered with a cold sweat. I saw a dim forecast of my future before my eyes. If it was true that the injection would make me confess, then I would be placing in jeopardy the lives of hundreds of people in the ghetto as well as others outside who had helped us out. I decided that the only solution was to kill myself. There was very little time to carry out my decision since the officer would appear shortly to put the chains back on me. So I found an appropriate spot on the ceiling, knotted my belt and started to write a farewell note to my parents, my sister and brother and all my friends. I don't know if I can communicate my condition and feelings at that moment.

Suddenly the police officer entered to put my chains on and saw immediately that something unusual was going on and immediately put me into the chains. Then he grabbed the letter I had written and brought it to the bureau upstairs. They must have found a Jew to translate it, since it was written in Yiddish, and the chief realized he was not likely to get from me the information he wanted. He then changed his mind. He was ready at that point to take money in order for me to be freed. There ensued a chain of circumstances that take on the character of a history of martyrdom. At one point it was decided that I and several others would be hanged in our ghetto. But as a result of a number of circumstances I was able to escape that fate. I won't go into detail about that because I don't want to be considered a martyr. Ultimately I was set free on the condition that I leave Strzegowo and its environs as quickly as possible.

The only feasible alternative was for me to go to Warsaw. Near Mlawa, in a town called Nosarzhava, there was a large work camp. The head of the camp indicated that for a large amount of money he would drive me across the provincial borders to Warsaw. A friend from Mlawa, Moyshe David Frankel who now lives in Germany, was also in the car and on the way we were stopped by the Gestapo, arrested and sent to Plotsk. Whether the Gestapo had been informed or whether it was just an accident is something I don't know to this day.

After being in jails in several cities, I was finally sent to Auschwitz in the summer of 1942.

When I left Strzegowo all the sanctions against ghettos were also enforced there. Twenty Jews were hanged in the ghetto. The entire

population of the ghetto, in a brutal action was shipped to Auschwitz. When the Jews arrived there, I was already an old inmate and
had many connections. I got word about when they were supposed
to arrive because the transports came in a regular order city by city.
I thought I would have one last meeting with my beloved Strzegowo compatriots before we died. But it was not to be. The Strzegowo transport with men, women, and children was sent immediately to the gas chambers. Only about four or five people escaped
into the camp.

All the rest were immediately gassed. In the most horrible and
painful moments, their spirits were sent on high.

BEN-ZION BOGEN

The End of the Jews
in Strzegowo

On 4 September, that is four days after the outbreak of war, the Hitlerite armies took over our little town of Strzegowo.[9] Shortly after they arrived, many of the homes in the town were destroyed as a result of the bombardment that took place on the very first day of the occupation. Strzegowo was one of those towns in central Poland that was originally German, so hell broke loose there earlier than in some other parts of the country. Very quickly, then, the ethnic Germans who were living in towns nearby quickly became the bosses. As soon as they were given weapons, they began to get wild in the town quite on their own: it involved robbery, beatings, and grabbing people for work. They immediately threw the inhabitants out of their homes and moved in themselves. They took over the furniture, clothing, and even the bedding. There were times when they attacked Jews in the street and stole their boots. Some people who could see what was coming gave many of their valuables to Gentile neighbors and asked them to hide them away. Nothing was ever retrieved.

The ethnic Germans simply took the Jews for their slaves. Since it was fall, the Jews had to dig potatoes, beets, and other products from the fields. They exempted no one and took old and young alike to the fields. They took special pleasure in tormenting older, orthodox people like the *shoykhet*. Knowing that those people were not able to do physical labor, since they spent most of their lives studying, they gave them especially difficult assignments. One of

9. Much of the information recounted here was gathered by the author from the Polish inhabitants of Strzegowo. [F. M.]

the results was that the Strzegowo Jews were quickly reduced to wearing rags, torn and dirty clothing. At first the use of Jews for labor was chaotic rather than organized, and consequently, it was possible for some people to hide from their slave masters. But later, in line with the German character, they became organized, and no one could escape the assignments. On the way to work in the fields themselves, people were regularly beaten. The most brutal were the ethnic Germans.

The First Pogrom

In a short time, when the German administration was established, the ethnic Germans carried out pogroms against several of the local shops. They threw the contents on the street and trod all over them. What was left they instructed the Gentiles to remove. You can be sure there was no lack of takers. After they stole what they wanted, they began to beat several of the proprietors and one of their young children. They took them to a nearby woods and with the pretext that they were "abnormal," they were all shot.

I looked in vain for their bodies and even offered ten thousand zlotys for anyone who could locate them. I and a few other survivors intended to exhume the bodies and give them a Jewish burial. As was the case with all the people in German occupied territory, we were given by the Hitlerites a special insignia to wear: it was a yellow cloth with a Star of David on it. It was to be worn by all men and women on their clothes, just above the breast.

The Role of the Judenrat

The Judenrat consisted of Ben-Zion Bogen, Khana Stavitsky, Yudel Stavitsky, Barukh Rebek, Feldman from Rotshoynu, and several other Jews who had been driven into Strzegowo from nearby towns. They were billeted in Roden's house. Their role was to carry out the orders that were given by the Hitlerites. They also created the Jewish police, made a census of the population in the ghetto, and were ordered to collect contributions from the people. Among their responsibilities was putting men and women to various work assignments. Often people were sent to Mlawa to work because the Strzegowo ghetto was officially connected with the one there. Most of the police were recruited from young people who came from Sherpts. Also, the head of the police was someone from Sherpts who was killed by the Germans at the train station during one of the deportations of Strzegowo Jews. I was unfortunately not able to get his name.

The Origins of the Ghetto

On 6 January 1941, the Germans ordered that Strzegowo be walled in and a ghetto created. It was ordered that the ghetto be established in the area near the pig market and environs. The western boundary of the ghetto was near the road to Mlawa, the eastern boundary was near Calvin's field, the northern boundary was near where Joshua Dombrover and Gutmorgen lived, and the southern side was where the houses ended near the pig market. The ghetto was completely walled in, and the entrance was near Dombrover and Kviatkowsky's house. A number of the Jewish police kept watch at the door and regulated the flow of those people going out to work and those who entered. The signal for those who needed to go out to work was given by a bell. That was the indication that the people needed to assemble. The Germans didn't like the way it was handled, thinking it took too long. So they decided to do it their own way, which meant that they urged people on by beating them with sticks. More than once during these procedures, Jewish victims were seriously injured.

The work consisted mainly of repairing roads, rebuilding a German cement works, and other improvement projects. Jewish women were used to clean houses for the Germans, sweep streets, and clean the market place. Among the most difficult tasks for the women was their responsibility in summer to lie on the ground and pick blades of grass from the market place. All this was under the control of the Judenrat and the Jewish police. It stands to reason that there were favorites as well as victims. As in all the ghettos, the Strzegowo Judenrat was very much under the influence of the Germans, thinking that if they carried out the orders rigorously there would be a better chance for their own survival. Ultimately, however, all the members of the *Judenrat* met the same fate as the other inhabitants of the town, with the one exception of Ben-Zion Bogen.

No one knows why, but the Nazis brought many Jews into our Ghetto from Sherpts, Byezhon, Drobin, and even from places much farther away. The Strzegowo ghetto alone contained fourteen hundred souls. With the addition of the many deportees from other towns, the total was much, much higher. I'm not exactly sure of the figures, but ultimately there were as many as four thousand Jews in the Strzegowo ghetto.

Life in the Ghetto

Life in the ghetto was dreadful. Even the smallest room there held at least eight people. There was hardly any place for anyone to sit down. There were even people living in Dombrover's granary. Understandably, sanitary conditions were in a sad condition. With lightning speed, a typhus epidemic occurred and there was hardly a day that did not claim several victims of the disease. There were no Jewish doctors and no medicines. The town's lay surgeon [*feldsher*], Saltzberg, had died before the ghetto was established.

There was a Jewish pharmacist from another town who had some medicine and helped people. Hearing that there was a pharmacist in the ghetto, the Nazis sought him out and beat him viciously with their rifle butts until he died. As I said, there was no medication, and the only cure available was water. After the epidemic was well under way and many had already died, the *Judenrat* received permission to establish a hospital. It was set up in the Klinyevskys' house, and each patient had barely enough space to lie on the floor. The Polish doctor, Grochowsky, was allowed to visit the ghetto hospital, but there was nothing he could do to save anyone. His typical visit involved taking someone's pulse and predicting, more or less, when the patient would die.

It was strictly forbidden for the Jews to gather in groups of any kind. The Nazis circulated through the ghetto, peering into the windows of the houses. When they saw several people together, they immediately opened fire. The ethnic Germans as well as the Poles often came into the ghetto drunk and carried out various "maneuvers." This took place mostly late at night. They often took groups of Jews and ordered them to fight among themselves. When they had fallen exhausted to the ground, the tormentors threw water on them, and when they revived they were sometimes taken just outside the door and shot. This awakened more inhabitants and also provided more victims.

There were signs of unrest among the youth, who began to bridle under the regulations imposed on them. There was one occasion when an ethnic German demanded that a young girl come to him to be tortured. She refused to obey and was instantly shot. Seeing that she was still alive, he approached and shot her point-blank in the chest. She was twenty years old and was a deportee from Bezoyn. I don't actually recall her name.

There was another occasion when a group of young men, fearing that they would be conscripted for labor and tortured, decided to run from the ghetto in the direction of the town of Alexandrowa, where they hid in the fields. When the Germans saw this they went in pursuit and encircled the field. Not one of the young men emerged alive. Later on the Nazis regaled the local Gentiles with stories about how well they shot on that occasion.

The Nazis decided that Mendl and Benyomin Zheloni were guilty of left-wing sympathies. On a clear day they were taken from the ghetto, and I have never been able to discover where they were taken to be killed.

The son-in-law of David Tiks escaped from the Warsaw ghetto and came to Strzegowo. He brought the frightening news that the Jews who were being deported from the ghettos were being gassed to death. How this news was circulated among the Gentiles as well, I can't say. But the fact is that they as well as the Germans in town were also aware of the procedures. The Germans quickly arrested him, threw him into a cellar, and later hanged him. The local Gentiles told me that he was strangled. The teachers Abraham Binem

Margolin and Yitzkhak Friedman operated a religious school in the ghetto. This became an obvious place where the Nazis could exercise their sadistic pleasures. Often they fell upon the children in the *kheder* and beat them mercilessly. There were times when the children jumped from the windows to evade the Nazis' beatings.

The situation concerning food in the ghetto was a terrible one. Only a minimal amount of food was brought into the ghetto. A few loaves of bread and some spoiled milk from the dairy was a standard menu. From time to time we were given a little meat from a dead horse. You can imagine that under these conditions, people were willing to risk their lives to escape from the ghetto to smuggle in some food. If any such person was caught on the Gentile side, he was instantly shot. Melekh Izerovitch and Raphael Levinsky were a little luckier: they died in a dungeon after being tortured for a few weeks . . .

The Gentiles who brought food to the ghetto asked for outlandish prices, with the result that they received much gold and other valuables. It happened often that a Jewish woman gave away her wedding ring for a loaf of bread, or golden chains and other precious objects.

From day to day the situation grew worse and soon there was nothing left to buy. Every day there were new restrictions, every day more victims of shootings and deaths from hunger.

A Gruesome Sight

The sixth of August 1942 was a terrible day for all the Jews in the Strzegowo ghetto. On that day the Judenrat received an order that all Jews should assemble. When all were together, a Gestapo officer read aloud a list of those who were to be arrested and put to death. He read the following names:

Leib Goldstein, 65 years of age
Avigdal Tiks, 38 years of age
Gedalye Tiks, 30 years of age
Rubin Izerovitch, 43 years of age

Eliezer Izerovitch, 48 years of age
Jacob Goldstein, 25 years of age
Abraham Binem Margolin, 66 years of age
Yekhiel Plaut, 28 years of age
Simkhe Rebek, 30 years of age
Nakhman Greenberg, 25 years of age
Faivl Brievtreger, 19 years of age
Khaim Shurek, 30 years of age
Hirsh Garfinkel, 27 years of age
Yikhzekl Fass, from Sherpts
Joseph Ephraim Lelonek, from Sherpts
Tobias Zhitelni, from Sherpts
Malevyok, from Byezhon
and two unknown people – twenty persons in all.

All of them were thrown into a dungeon and the Jewish police were strictly warned not to allow any of their relatives to see them. It's hard to imagine how they were able to sustain themselves there without food or water. All of them were sentenced to death by the Nazis, and the dungeon was to be the appointed place, in order to prevent any disturbances by their relatives. In addition to the Jewish police, the Germans also guarded the prisoners. But sometimes when the Germans weren't looking it was possible to get close to the cellar. It was not possible to get food to them, but one could pray nearby. And others read Mishnaic sayings, as if they were already dead. In that area there were some pitiful scenes enacted – mothers came and some even cut their veins. For four weeks they lay in the dungeon, and from time to time Nazis from Mlawa came to see if they were still in condition to be executed.

The day before the execution was to be carried out, the area around the dungeon was sealed off with barbed wire and the victims brought out of the cellar. Standing behind the wire, they were forced to watch as the gallows was constructed about five meters from the dungeon. The Jews of the ghetto had to bring wood and stones for the gallows. Several Jews were beaten while practicing how to remove the stools from under the victims' feet. At a command, they had to carry the stools in and then, in response to another command, remove them quickly from under the feet of the prisoners. On the second of September 1942, while it was still dark in the morning, the Jews of Strzegowo, men, women, and children, were forced to assemble near the gallows. Then they had to set up chairs for the ethnic Germans, who came happily with their wives and children. The Germans laughed raucously and explained to their children that when they were grown up it was their responsibility also to kill Jews. Around eleven o'clock, three Gestapo men arrived from Mlawa to carry out the executions. The hands and feet of each of the prisoners were bound and the nooses placed around their necks. One of the Gestapo men explained why each one was being executed. One was accused of sneaking out of the ghetto; another of smuggling food; Jacob Goldstein was accused of playing a Polish tune that encouraged the others to think of freedom.

When Khaim Shurek was already bound and had a chance to look at the crowd, he spied his wife and their three-year-old child by her side. In a few minutes' time, all twenty of the saintly men gave up the ghost. They remained strung up until six o'clock that night. Then they were cut down and taken to the forest near Calvin's land and buried in a mass grave that had been prepared earlier.

On 22 January 1948, the twenty sacrificial victims were exhumed from their mass grave and given a proper Jewish burial.

From that sorrowful day, there was never any doubt that all the Jews of Strzegowo would be liquidated. Everyone was completely unnerved and no one even bothered to undress before going to sleep. They were prepared for the worst at all times.

It finally came on 20 November 1942. That night there was an order that the Jews should assemble in the ghetto. The Nazis selected the old men and women, and in peasant carts that had been prepared they were all removed to the Mlawa ghetto. When they arrived there, the Gestapo were waiting and began beating them. Then with another contingent of Mlawa Jews they were all transported to the train station. Amidst hellish cries from the Nazi guards and the sobbing of children, they were ferociously driven into the railroad cars. Anyone who fell never arose again – he or she was immediately shot. Peasants recall that the entire way from Mlawa to the station was strewn with corpses. It's said that the transports on that day went directly to one of the worst death camps, Belshetz, where all were killed in the gas chambers there.

Four days later, 24 November 1942, the final evacuation of the Strzegowo ghetto took place. This time all the Jews without exception had to assemble in the ghetto. They were transported in peasant carts directly to the train station in Mlawa. Under a hail of blows and fusillades of bullets, the Jews were driven into the freight cars, which had been sprayed with chloroform that cut into their eyes.

As many as 240 people were smashed together in one car. It was so crowded that some people were propelled into the air. There were some totally wild Germans at the train station who simply shot randomly into the wagons. The train arrived at Auschwitz, but there were already fewer people alive in the cars than when they started. Most of them died from the overcrowding and suffocation. There were some luckier ones who had quantities of poison and took their own lives. As it was described to me by one of the officials from the town administration of Strzegowo, two hundred Jews had died from starvation and typhus in the ghetto itself.

Later Information

In the ghetto there were some philanthropic activities carried out, in which richer individuals used their money to help some of the less affluent people. But it didn't actually help very much. It turned out that even though money was collected, there was nothing left to buy.

I was informed about another episode. During the transfer of the Jews to Mlawa, two managed to escape and ran in the direction of the river near the mill. The Nazis pursued them and they jumped into the water. The river was frozen, but their attempt to be free gave them such strength that they were able to swim among the ice floes to the opposite shore. But there were other murderers waiting for them there and they opened fire on the unfortunates. Wounded and bloodied, they threw themselves into the water again. I never found out what their names were.

According to my information only select individuals managed to survive in Auschwitz. The foregoing description describes how a beloved town in Poland was liquidated – Strzegowo.

Strzegowo People in the Warsaw Ghetto

It was in the month of November 1939, after the German troops marched into Poland, that Strzegowo was annexed to the Third Reich. A second part, including Warsaw, was proclaimed to be a section of the overall government. During that time, some families from Strzegowo managed to get across the border and establish themselves in Warsaw. The plan was to see if life would be better in Warsaw and if so to bring the rest to them. And on the other hand, if conditions were better in Strzegowo, the first group would arrange to sneak back. Everything turned out to be quite different. There was no chance for the people in Strzegowo to escape to Warsaw. And there was no way for the people in Warsaw to come back. The terror and torture of the Nazi invasion was the same everywhere. Those who came to Warsaw were the following: my parents, Joseph and Manye Meirantz; Rivke Shapiro and family; the Piotrikowsky family; Yitzkhak Scavron; Mendel Gutmorgen and family; Bela Perlmutter; Abba Novogrodsky and wife; Rabbi Simyatitsky and his wife and youngest son, Aaron; Mordkhe Berlin and family; David Tiks and his son, Tobias; Jacob Jacobovich and family; Shloyme Rosen and his wife; and the wife of Pyekhotka. The people from Strzegowo lived with relatives and friends in Warsaw.

Their Life in the Warsaw Ghetto

I often met the people from Strzegowo in the Shapiros' house where they all got together. They lived at Fukurny, number seven, which was on the south side of the ghetto. That was near the street that led to the Gdansk railroad station, where the trains from Mlawa and Ciechenow used to arrive. Between the two is where Strzegowo was. On entering the door, everyone from Strzegowo used to send a glance in the direction of the town, until the tears blocked out their vision.

Before the ghetto was closed, Aaron Shapiro used to look early in the morning in the direction of the Gdansk station to see if he could recognize any Poles from Strzegowo or nearby towns to find out what was happening there. Often he did find someone from the area and inquired about everyone and everything and thus got news about the trouble in Strzegowo. It developed that people from Strzegowo in all parts of the Warsaw ghetto came regularly to Shapiros' house. Everyone brought the latest gruesome news from the town. Rivke Shapiro was always the most pessimistic. After every report she would remark, "It's a pity. We will never survive the Hitler murderers."

Weeks and months passed and finally the ghetto was completely enclosed. Aaron Shapiro was no longer able to get information, since they were totally walled in. The small amount of food that people had brought from Strzegowo was fast running out. There were many days when we had not even a bite of bread to eat. We lived on the rationed water we received. People became weaker and weaker, suffering from hunger.

The second winter was approaching and there was no fuel of any kind left, so we lay in our beds, which accomplished two things: first to slake our hunger a bit and also to keep us a little warm. As with everyone else, the situation at the Shapiros' also changed. Feigl became ill, and since there was no medicine and hardly any food, she soon passed away. Rivke and Surtchen managed to get back to Strzegowo. When they said goodbye she noted: "It doesn't make any difference where you die. What's certain is that we will not survive." From that day onward, the Shapiros' house ceased to be the address for all of those from Strzegowo. And Aaron himself, making the rounds of the typhus victims like a reliable soldier, contracted the disease himself and soon sent his enlightened soul to heaven.

A little while later, as I was wandering in the cemetery, I came upon Aaron's grave and noticed that the inscription on it was in my father's handwriting. I wrote a new one and took the one of my father's since it was the only memory I had of him, that inscription in his own hand.

Those who were able to return to Strzegowo were: Mordkhe Berlin and family; Mendel Zelig and wife; and Shloyme Rosen. Yitzkhak Scovran went to Sukotshin, where he had a daughter, and Bela Perlmutter went to Mlawa. They all perished in the camps where they were taken.

From time to time I ran into some of the others who remained in the ghetto. My father had left me addresses, times, and dates when I should visit them. From one meeting to another, people became totally changed. The horror of the ghetto could be seen on every face – pale, gray, swollen from hunger, their bodies bent and weak. All suffered alike from cold and hunger. The terrible conditions were stamped on every visage. There was a constant longing for our old town but one's strength grew weaker and weaker.

My Last Visit to the Warsaw Ghetto
The last time I saw Rabbi Simyatitsky of Strzegowo in the ghetto it was hard to recognize him. He was totally undone, not so much from hunger, because that had become an accepted condition. It was rather from an article that he had read in the Nazi newspaper, *The Third Reich*, which stated directly that "All the Jews must be liquidated."

The news about the final solution quickly spread throughout the ghetto. At that time I realized that the next time I came to the ghetto, the rabbi would no longer be alive. And that was actually the case – he simply couldn't endure that news. He died a natural death. David Tiks also died at that time.

The rest of the Strzegowo people barely held out under the terrible circumstances, some dying sooner, and some dying later. Those who were sent to Treblinka and died there were: my parents, Abba Novgorodsky and his wife; Nakhum Jacobowsky, his wife and son, and the Piotrikowsky family. Those who perished during the Warsaw ghetto uprising and the last liquidation were: Helene Jacobowsky; Aaron Yoyne Simyatitsky; and Tobias Tiks. During the uprising Hinde Berlin's mother died a natural death. In Auschwitz, from the first selection there perished Abramik Piotrikowsky and Anshel Piotrikowsky's youngest son. Those who survived the Warsaw ghetto were Molly Piotrikowsky and her daughter, who managed to get to the Gentile quarter. Also Moyshe Gips, who lost a hand, and Hinde Berlin and I, Fishl Meirantz, survived the concentration camps.

This was a tragic chapter in human history, which I and a few others have managed to survive and retell so that it would not be forgotten.

FISHL MEIRANTZ

The Pain and Heroism of the Jews in Strzegowo

We people from Strzegowo in the ghetto stuck together.[10] We felt obligated to see one another, to transmit from one to another everything necessary so that not even for one day we should lose our close relationship, and all of us with our little town. All our intimate and important issues were taken care of by Aaron Shapiro and Aaron Yoine Simyatitsky [the rabbi's youngest son], and to a lesser extent myself. We three were occupied with all the issues and were concerned to help in all possible ways all those exiled from our neighboring towns who found themselves in Warsaw living in the most dreadful conditions; they lived in a variety of places in awful locations. Those in the worst shape were the Rotshoyners, who were living with five or six families in one room. As a result of dirt and hunger their numbers decreased every day.

It was most horrible to see the children in pain, their stomachs swollen from hunger, falling in the streets or being shot for smuggling a bit of bread or some potatoes. The same thing was taking place in our town.

Aaron Shapiro did everything he could to help out: he went to see the sick in various locations until he himself was infected with typhus, and on the sixth day of his sickness finally died. I first saw him when he began to lose his sense of being with us. Those closest to him were not permitted to see him for fear that they might also become infected with typhus. His death was for us Strzegower in Warsaw a great blow, and especially for Simyatitsky.

10. This was written in the DP camp at Belsen, 10 December 1948. Hinde Berlin ultimately escaped and now lives in the United States.

After the deaths of many Strzegower – David Tik, Aaron Shapiro, Simyatitsky, Miriam Piotrikowsky – there was a sense of bewilderment among us. Every day things got worse and our group grew smaller and smaller. Those remaining from Sherpts and other towns were captured and sent to the camps. All that were left were Simyatitsky and me; he was not able to survive more pain. Stuck in hiding in a dark cellar, he ventured out to come and say goodbye and prepare to be also sent away, with the full knowledge that he was about to be liquidated. He hoped to receive one more time some bread and marmalade.

I don't have any clear memories of those times. This was to be a last action, he knew very well – there would be no more bread, he would be dispatched without bread, so he hurried to see me once more. I couldn't look at events in that light. My mother was still alive at that time, and I couldn't bear to see her shot or tortured. Money or gold could no longer at that time postpone death even for one day. One couldn't buy time for even one day. So my mother and I went from one cellar to another to hide ourselves until the end of May in 1943. Several days before I was arrested our house – Muranovski 44 – was burned to the ground. Two days before the fire, like a saint, my mother died a natural death.

Because we weren't willing to simply give ourselves up, a group of Strzegower people were condemned to be shot. But they thought that was too light a sentence so we were loaded onto horse wagons, after being beaten severely, and sent to Lublin and the Maidenek camp. In Maidenek, Mrs. Salberg, from home, met her two daughters, who both waited to receive my plate in order to lick any food left on it. They were later shipped off to Radom on a train. I was not then useful to them, being too thin, so I was not included in the shipment. At that point there remained from our own people in Warsaw I and two daughters of Einhorn who were coworkers with me at the publication, *Today*. After a short stay in Maidenek they also disappeared. I was then left completely alone. Before leaving Maidenek I received twenty-five lashes from the local camp leader – a sort of honor! And then after fourteen days standing for roll-call I was left without support, just myself, Hinde Berlin.

A short time later I was sent to Auschwitz. When I was sent from Maidenek to Auschwitz I was luckily not even able to feel the pain from the tattooing on my arm of the number, 49330. I was still imbued with the naive hope that I would at last be able to locate some of my dear ones. It was only when I saw the huge chimneys and realized that they were not connected to factories but were attached to ovens where people were dispatched, where my whole family were annihilated, where my friends and my whole town were immolated, and that all the Jews were destined to end there – it was only then that I gave up all hopes of finding anyone at all. I saw then how short my life was to be in Auschwitz. My dearest hope was to receive a bullet, in short to be shot. But that was just an illusion. Very few had such luck. You had to be unusually blessed to be shot in Auschwitz.

Once when I was not able to go to my work, I was sent to toil in the camp: I was sent to pull the grass not far from the electric barbed-wire where some men were working. From some distance a man kept yelling, "Hinde, Hinde!" By that time I had almost forgotten my own name. A terrified person always seeks to protect herself from beatings and finds it hard to imagine that anyone is calling her name. The women with whom I was working pointed their fingers at themselves, thinking perhaps it was they who were being summoned. The man who was yelling made it clear that it was not they who were being called. One of the women shook me a bit – "It's you they are calling for," she said. Not believing her, I nevertheless raised my head and through the wire I saw a man calling – "Hinde, Hindele Berlin!"

When I asked him who he was, I could barely hear him say, "Klapman!" I wanted to ask him many more things, but a choking sob robbed me of speech and I was returned to my block with a confused understanding. After a short time for rest I was once again taken to the wire.

I swore my coworker to be silent, even in the worst circumstance not to let a tear drop but just to continue working. She was a person with feeling. Very soon I saw people running and recognized Yitzkhak Fabian, Yakov Finkelstein and from a distance, Hershl Rosen. I couldn't control myself then and started to yell to them, "Where are the rest, where is Mordkhe, my brother?" More can't be written on paper, perhaps you will not believe any more; and there may not be a place left in your imagination for any more of this tale.

They did everything they could to prevent me from dying of hunger. I pleaded with them on many occasions and refused to accept their help until they would tell me where my brother, Mordkhe, had been taken. He had been selected with the group to do the dirty and vile work they were forced to do. They chose from a few thousand men only family men for the work, including my brother. The assignment came under the heading of Sonder Commando – that is, they were to burn in the crematoria those many people who had been gassed to death. But he was not able to survive such a task, even if his own life was at stake. He simply could not exist in such a hell to burn people not guilty of any sin, his own women, children, parents, sisters, and brothers; to burn people and whole towns – such a hell had not ever been imagined by any human being. To choose from thousands the individuals who were commanded to exterminate their dearest and closest relatives. Such a task my brother, Mordkhe Berlin, was not able to perform, despite the views of the others who tried to prevent him from even thinking of going with the innocents into the gas chamber and being cremated thereafter. Mordkhe could foresee that if there ever would come a time to take revenge, he might be too far gone and become like those others who had forgotten their holy vows and begun to feel little hatred and thus be incapable of ever taking revenge – who had forgotten the horrible pain they had seen. And if it meant becoming such a demented person, with no memory, with no remembrance, it would be better even if healthy, to go to his death in the gas chambers.

That is what he thought and that is what he did, without consulting with anyone. He only did the work for a short time and became increasingly confused. Just before I arrived there was a selection – that is, of victims.

Chosen were those who were no longer capable of any work, and they were to be taken to be eliminated. Mordkhe, who was at the time healthier and more capable of working than many others, placed himself close to those already chosen for death. He could have been saved, but he would not be thwarted from his plan. Blessed be his thoughts!

When he was still in Strzegowo he wanted to organize a partisan group, but our forests were too small to conceal them and the number of Christian anti-Semites was too great.

I quickly accepted the idea of his death, being sure that in a short time the same fate would befall me as well. Then my Strzegower together determined not to let me die of hunger. They somehow managed to send medication for me and many others whose wounds needed to be healed. Every possible form of help was sent to me.

Yitzkhak Fabian was the most helpful. They found special oils and sent them to the women in order to heal their scabies. It was extremely difficult to send those forbidden items, but I distributed them to a great many, medicine to prolong their lives for a while.

A little while later, Klapman, Lisa Pashitzki, Yakov Finkelstein (who was in fairly good shape in the camp as a hairdresser) were all sent off to the gas chambers. Yakov's last words in his letters were: "I know that I'm being sent to my death. It's all the same to me what my fate will be, as long as I'm free of Auschwitz and the Sonder Commandos. Blessed are those who have not done what I did." Very soon we found out where they and the three hundred other healthy and capable men were taken.

After a while some of the Sonder Commandos were working strongly at their covert work. At that time in Auschwitz three young women were hanged, among them a particular woman from Strzegowo, a cousin of Stavitzky's. The young women were working in an ammunition factory, called Union. While dealing with the fallout of ammunition powder, they managed to smuggle portions out. Our Yitzkhak Fabian was one of the activists involved. Everything I knew I got from him, except for the details of the preparations to blow up the crematoriums – this last he kept as a secret to himself. Every letter that he sent me placed his life at risk, but nevertheless every day we exchanged some information. The way we accomplished this is not possible to be described. We saw each other from a distance through small openings in the wires and often recognized each other through various codes. The last time we saw each other was just before Yom Kippur, 1944. He came at that time to the women's camp as a sewer worker. In order to see me and talk things over he advised me to be on the alert to escape at the precise moment when the electric barbed-wire would be cut. It was a lucky sign when several days earlier there came to us in the women's camp as a doctor with a Red Cross box, a certain Pitel from Mlawa who worked with the Sonder Commando; he was anxious to see those who had a connection with their comrades in the organization. My job at that time was to clean up the laundry rooms and the sewers, so that gave me an opportunity to see the men and Yitzkhak. That time, just before Yom Kippur, at our last meeting together, before he got a word out, there emerged as if from the earth itself a camp capo (an ethnic German woman), and with several blows she bloodied my entire face so that I could no longer see anything. It was only later that I was able to share several words with him. In his last letter to me (it probably still remains until today in a remote spot in a sewer hidden away), he wrote that I must continue to believe that freedom is coming soon.

About that time, when the uprising had been planned in all of its aspects, the camp leaders showed up and condemned some of the young men to the ovens. When the last group came and was expected to engage in the same checking of the ovens, a certain Jewish man from Bialystok, a provocateur, gave up all of our plans to the German camp leader. There was an immediate alarm, and the uprising that had already been planned was moved up a couple of hours. Not taking into account any provocation, the several men involved in the uprising, including our Yitzkhak Fabian from Strzegowo and Pital from Mlawa, set out to blow up the crematorium [there were actually four crematoria] and to cut the barbed-wire. Just at that moment the Hitler murderers let loose a hail of machine gun fire and our heroes met their death. The first to fall was Pital. Yitzkhak fell farther along in the field. That showed his strength and energy, something hundreds of thousands were not capable of against the Hitlerite bloody dogs.

Thus fell a group of our brave comrades in the fight for the honor of the Jewish people and our little town, Strzegowo.

It may be that it is too much to hear about the deaths of so many people. I will not beg any apologies from our readers for such discussions. Believe me when I say that life in Auschwitz was worse than death. One day of living there led us, on the next day, to wish to be undone – we saw clearly enough which death would release us from the hellish life, to be gassed and thrown into the fires of the crematoria. And that is the way our families were destroyed. That is the way our little town came to its end. That is the way our Warsaw was immolated. That is the way our Poland was ravaged and our six million Jews came to their fate.

Also the life in our Strzegowo ghetto was more horrible than can be described. Small and extremely crowded was the Strzegowo ghetto. There were only a few houses into which all the Jews from neighboring towns were driven – Radzhanov, Zhouramin, some of those fleeing from Rotshoyns, Byezhoun, Sherpts, and Drobin.

In order to remain a little longer in Strzegowo, the Jews gave up everything they had, everything that had been hidden all those years, even for decades. Involved in all this were our "friends" for many years, the ethnic Germans of the town with whom we lived for so many years, with whom we were brought up and went to school. They were suddenly the sources of ferocious bestiality toward us.

You Strzegowo folk surely must remember them, those whose celebrations were held, whose brothers find themselves today in America.

If in a Jewish house a little butter, or a little cornmeal, or an egg was found, there was the immediate threat of hanging. Every few days there were revisions of the rules. After each revision, the Jews were herded together in one place and their poor little packs inspected – whatever they had retained. They carried out a "control," passed some bad jokes, and then drove the Jews back into their houses. The most beautiful Jewish children, especially the young girls, were forced to do the dirtiest work. More and more they were driven to the filthiest assignments, as a result of the race hatred laws.

When I first heard these stories, I no longer wanted to know any more about it, and I can't even now write about it. I can't write any more about the pain of our victims, how they were hanged and driven from their homes; not even one was able to escape. I longed rather for death through gas and fire.

HINDE BERLIN

How My Daughter and I
Survived the Holocaust

How difficult it is to try to write something about the gray, tragic days we lived through. My whole family perished in the hell of the Warsaw ghetto at the hands of the Hitlerites. I was the only one of my father Yitzkhak Meir Piotrikowsky's children who survived the ordeal. My grief and pain are hard to describe. A pen is not rich enough to detail all the things I lived through during the Hitlerite occupation. I will nevertheless try to give some impressions here.

It is 1943. I was with my daughter, Branica, who remained with me after my saintly husband, Henekh Grossbard, delivered us to the "Aryan side." After a few weeks in the ghetto he was killed by the Hitlerite murderers.

We knew a Pole who was seriously interested in us. Those were difficult days. I didn't have a good approach to the place I was in, and I needed to leave the house where I had been staying. Confused as I was, I wandered around the streets, looking for a place where I could stay overnight. Suddenly I found myself surrounded by a gang of young Christian kids who began throwing stones at me and crying loudly, "Jewess! Jewess!"

The young children had obviously discovered that I was a Jew. Several of them wanted to steal my purse. I began to run away and they chased me. Some Polish police showed up and turned me over to the Germans. It was no surprise to me or my daughter that there was no way out at that point. The fate of any Jew who fell into the Germans' hands was known. But since we had in our possession the documents of Aryans, we decided to try to play the role of Christians. There was nothing to lose. We were taken and interrogated –

where did we come from? were we familiar with Christian prayers?

My daughter could answer all their questions. But I was not able to answer successfully. That wasn't good. The Germans were not at all certain that we were Christians. They were pretty well convinced that we were two Jewish women. They kept us overnight in detention. If during that time we were not able to find a Pole who knew us from before the war, they would have us in their clutches.

There was in fact one Polish friend that we had – just the one I mentioned above, named Pero, with whom we had earlier hidden ourselves. It was night, there was no telephone in his house, it was necessary to call him at his work place. It might be possible that he wasn't at work, and who could be sure that a Christian would want to rescue us, for he could forfeit his life by falsely testifying for us. But we had no choice. This was our last chance. There shot through our minds many different phone numbers. But we couldn't remember which one was Pero's. The Germans called – they seemed to be enjoying our confusion. We were lucky. The number we gave them was right, Pero was at work in his night job at a hotel. The question now was whether he would be too frightened to help us.

The German orderly spoke to him. She asks him if he knows the woman Piotrikowsky and her daughter. They had been identified as Jews, was he willing to swear that he knew them? If so, he should come to the jail in the morning where he would be interrogated. With inconceivable impatience and with fear in our hearts, we wait for the morning to come. Will he show up?

The Christian Pero did show up, though a little late. The Germans questioned him.

Yes, he says, he knew us during the time before the war as Christians. He can swear to it. The Germans ask him if he knows the punishment for false testimony. The Christian holds fast to his statements. He has nothing to fear. He speaks the truth. His memory is accurate. He speaks German well. The police believe him. We were cleared. Before they set us free, the Germans apologize for the false charges against us. They assure us that if we need help in any future situations we should be sure to come to them. After all, to be accused of being Jewish is no minor charge.

Pero gave us some money and helped us to get organized. Even though his own house was under observation, he brought us there and took care of us. There were actually some other Jews that he was keeping also. He took care of us to the very last minute.

Everyone who was hidden by him is alive today. He himself perished in the Warsaw Ghetto uprising in 1944.

That is how we survived and came to live in Israel.

MOLLY PIOTRIKOWSKY

Two Letters

Lignitz, Lower Silesia
25 January 1948

To the Secretary of the Strzegowo Landslait in America,
Feigl Bisberg-Youkelson:

Today after a week of traveling I have now returned home and write to you. When I mention traveling I mean back from the exhuming of the Strzegowo Jews, the victims who were hanged by the Hitlerites. I have written you about the details of the exhumation separately.

I have to admit that sitting here in Lower Silesia where I have seen a few Jews made me think that there must be many more, that the tragedy was not as bad as I thought. But when I traveled home I first saw how great was our loss. When we passed towns and cities where there were once Jewish settlements, people looked at us as if we had just come back from the other world. We didn't see even one Jewish house where we could sleep overnight – that showed us the total of Hitler's accomplishment.

When we arrived in our little town, Strzegowo, where we were born and raised, lived and made our lives, hoped and dreamed of a better world and enlightened future not only for us but for all humanity – only then could we see how horrible the catastrophe was.

In Strzegowo everything was as it had always been – the sun shone and smiled on the house of study where our fathers and mothers used to pour out their sorrows about a world that troubled them so. But now the little shul was abandoned and orphaned. How could the public look on and watch as parents hanged their own children and were then forced to bury them in a common grave, dressed in their ragged clothes and wooden shoes?

When I passed a house where one of our Jews used to live I

thought, now he will come out with his large beard and I will talk over old times with him, when there was a developing Jewish culture, when Jewish issues were alive. But suddenly a peasant appears and asks in his rough voice, "What do you want?" And my whole dream is dissolved. And if I go into a house where a Jew once lived I can see that in the place where there once hung a painting of Moses or of the Spanish Inquisition, now there are icons of Jesus and Mary. There were, however, some good people among the Polish folk.

It's impossible for me to write more. After my visit to Strzegowo I remain a person broken and confused. One thing I would underscore – the light of the Jews in Strzegowo is forever obscured. But in our memory it will forever burn brightly.

Lignitz, Lower Silesia
22 February 1948

Dear Feigl Bisberg-Youkelson:

You ask me to write to you about how our dearest and nearest relatives came to their end. I have to admit that I am too weak for that assignment. It has nothing to do with my writing talent; but simply that my heart could not take the strain. But I would say that if we sob over our dearest ones, it is only their gruesome death that we mark. But what I learned after returning to Strzegowo, where not one Jew remains alive, is that death was not for them so horrible. Rather it was for them a kind of deliverance. They begged for death.

The Hitlerite bandits did not give one a death so quickly. First one had to experience horrible pains – torture, hunger, deadly blows, and insults; they were half naked and barefoot – torn apart. At the same time, parents were forced to hang their own children and then were marched cruelly into the gas chambers.

But not all were so easily put to death. Many were forced to stand and wait in line until it was their turn to be burned in the crematoria.

I heard from a young Pole who came from Strzegowo and who worked with my youngest brother, Moyshele, who was one of the "lucky ones." They were sent to work outside the ghetto. The Pole was a chauffeur for the head of the Strzegowo ghetto. He told me that when the order came to take all the Jews to Volko and then from there transport them to Auschwitz, even the so-called lucky ones knew very well that they were on their last journey. The leader of the camp called my brother in to see him, to say goodbye and offer him some money. My brother refused to take the money. He said, "In the next world it's not necessary to have any money." The leader of the camp then told the Pole to give my brother six loaves of bread for the trip. The bread he took, saying he could use that for the Jews, for the whole family, until they all went to their deaths. The Pole told me that later, the head of the ghetto said, "What a pity that such an outstanding young man should be sent to his death in the ovens!"

My brother could have saved himself, but he chose not to. He chose to go to his death with his parents and all the rest of the Jews. He chose to die and be rid of his gruesome and unbearable life.

I can write no more. My heart bursts with pain and sorrow. And please forgive me for writing so much about my heroic brother. I have no egotistic motives there. Blessed be his memory and the others who fell at the hands of the Hitlerites.

Beinush Vure
Israel

Strzegowo Lives in
My Imagination

Life has its own rules. The order is not instituted in its own way, as if by experienced engineers. Every individual, as a member of a family, plays his or her own role in their time. But at the same moment, the individual takes his place within the ranks of the family life. There also come in time certain changes. For instance, individuals are born, that is to say, from time to time a person comes into the family. People die, that is to say, from time to time, one loses a member of the family. These facts result in joy or sorrow, but in the long run things turn out evenly. The family on the whole is like a tree with roots deep in the earth and many branches on the stem. Sometimes a root dries up, sometimes a branch dies. There is always a balance of roots and branches. Sometimes, for various reasons, all the roots are poisoned, and the juices of the tree stop nurturing all the branches; or the roots in one fell swoop are exterminated, and even the lightest wind that no one even noticed affects it or does away with it entirely.

It was just such a fate that recently overtook the whole of European Jews. When the extermination of the six million tore away whole families and the exceptions who remained, whether they emerged alive from the Holocaust or whether they had earlier escaped from Europe, they were in fact unbalanced. Not only their tears but their nerves were not in any normal condition. Even the smallest occurrence throws them off balance. And sometimes without any reason they awake from sleep completely unnerved. The main sign of such a condition is that the individuals remained absolutely without roots. No one could look back to the ethnic distance, when everyone lived with mother and father, sister and brother. In thought, we lived with them, celebrated with them, shared their holidays. Suddenly, in one action, it all stopped. A person looks around and sees that in one terrible act all the roots are chopped down, and one begins to shake and sees that from that time one has lost his balance. I am one of those people.

Once in the middle of the night, as if someone had delivered a blow to my head with a hammer, I suddenly was awakened. Was there a reason? Somewhere a gentle wind almost unnoticed had given the tree without roots a shaking. Loss of sleep is the most painful thing. I jumped out of bed and went out on the terrace. There something enveloped me with such a warm feeling. I raised my eyes and saw a blazing moon set in a sky with pale stars. I rejoiced with them as if they were an old and almost intimate friend. And that warm feeling led me as if by an invisible hand to the well of an old-fashioned warmness, to Strzegowo – my little town of Strzegowo.

The moon is such a good friend, like the inhabitants of my poor, poor little town, without electric lights, who are satisfied with the pale moonlight of such nights. People from larger towns ignore the moon and prefer the crying and *khutzpa* of electric light. But not I, from this small town, where the moon was so precious to me all these years, until I left it. So now when I think about my Strzegowo town, I think of it always at night, under the sky and moon, because sunlight is the same everywhere, in Tel Aviv as in Strzegowo.

As if talking with an old friend, I found myself talking to the moon about my Strzegowo. I forgot entirely the tragic facts. Everything was different in the looking back, as if I once again were reliving it, or to say it better, as if I turned back and saw it from a few years ago.

I relived everything, but it was different. The time cut was working, and from everyone, perspective-wise, I saw among them well-known people of Strzegowo; special sides of each one of the members of the community were shown to me, special times and moments of their lives. That's just the one. And more.

During the day, everyone was busy with his own occupation. This was done in a small town way, but still professionally. One could always have a little chat with someone, but the main thing was to get on with the work. In the evening everyone had his or her own life to lead, each one opening clearly his or her own personality. In any case, the moon brought me close to the people of Strzegowo, and every vision that I saw was as if I was looking through a magnifying glass and thinking about the main characteristics of each one I saw. And also I saw each one so clearly as if I knew them well. That night, the moon reconstructed my poor and lost town. There developed before my eyes a picture of a wonderful night when in the light of the moon I remembered my town. Strzegowo. Still. Evening. In the light of every lit-up window sits someone, reading a newspaper or a book.

In the streets there are groups of people meandering, young boys and young girls. They are walking from the center of the town to the market and back. From one of these promenading groups, a couple is paired off, walking slowly and dreaming. One hears little of their talk. They pause on the bridge, looking at the water that surrounds them, though they see absolutely nothing. Only their hearts speak. And they understand very well these voices of their souls. And when after a long silence they begin to talk, it is as if secrets are told, witnessed by the waves and the rush of the grasses on the nearby shores. One can hear the sounds of wedding vows . . .

The stars in the sky wink to each other like curious children who have seen something mysterious. But the good-natured moon shakes its head and says: "Silly children. There's nothing new here. This is an old story." Every young couple is sure that this display of honest, true love is their own discovery. But at a later time their own children will have exactly the same thoughts.

Among the shops and homes, the fathers of the loving couple that we saw near the waters are also present and carry on a lively discussion, dealing with their prosaic lives – about dowries and attendants. The promenade on the highway or on the streets goes on. In the market place there are many interesting personalities, and I see them clearly before my eyes; and seeing them thus I feel shivers in my body. Each one is such a special type. Living with and near them, it all comes to this: Strzegower Jews – but now, as if emerging from a mist. I see particular types, and when one comes nearer to me, I see him as if projected and I can recognize a singular character . . .

In the whole swarm of promenading characters and the many-sided content of their conversations – politics, parties, literature, and, of course, a little gossip – a figure shows itself in the shadows. I look carefully and see it is Elia Grotch. He walks back and forth, deep in thought. Yes, in thought, an ordinary person, and yet there's something special about him. In the summer he's selling orchards, and in midwinter he's selling grains, and in between he's a tailor and concerned with the problems of children. If the truth be told, however, his problems soon took on real forms. In a characteristic way he concerned himself with the problems of the poor, in just the ways that no one else paid any attention to. For example, he was worried about the problems of poor people who lacked *matzo* and wine for Passover, and collected money in order to give the poor potatoes, a little meat, and some fat. And in time he was concerned not only with Passover but for all the holidays. And the more he got involved, the more he was able to feel just where the needs were and how people were affected. It was as if he took off the clothing of his own self and was attentive rather to those who were in need.

In addition to that, he was a person with a great talent for humor and for making up verses of poetry. His greatest pleasure was to appear at a wedding as a *batkhen*. He was a *batkhen* and he made up verses. And the verses kept pouring out of him, one after the other. From such a person, without any education, it was an amazing thing to behold.

When I think about him, I realize that in such a character, an artist was lost. He was the kind of individual who took occurrences seriously, felt them in his soul, and attempted to clothe them in verse. Of course, all this was done in his head, by heart and not on paper. It brings to mind something that happened many years ago, in 1922, when my aunt Gitele died at a very young age. In such a small town, it made a lasting imprint. Such a young woman dead, and having left behind small children. In the soul of Elia Grotch this made such an impact that he dedicated a piece to her. For him it was necessary to create a poem. Of course, he took care not to tell anyone what he was doing, except me, a young boy then who was touched personally by the tragedy. When I think about it, I wonder that he was able to bring it about, that he could picture the tragedy of the house with such feeling as it was disturbed by the event and he sang: "How often I came here to slaughter a hen and never imagined it would be the end." It was a moving expression.

A person winds his way through the market place. I recognize him: it is Mordkhe Lanke. An old man but with a youthful stride and short, quick steps. Why is he in such a hurry? He smokes his pipe and rushes home. He is in such a hurry because he's anxious to look into the pages of a very secular book. It is his biggest pleasure to lose himself in such a book. Those stories had a great impact on him; he lived so fully in them. He once decided to take up the heroes of those stories, where those stories are also fully described. Once he took up the stories with courage and brought them to the house of study, where he questioned Reb Moyshe, the *shoykhet*: "Ahem, ahem," he said, "Moyshele, do me a favor. I hear how the sages study here the Gemara, and they say that Rubin borrowed money from Simon and refused to pay back the loan. And Levi has stolen money from Yehuda. Moyshele, how can that be, that Rubin, Simon, and Levi, such saintly people, the children of Jacob, should steal and borrow and not pay back the loan? How can that be? Ahem, ahem."

Moyshele *shoykhet*, as he was called, answered him good-naturedly: "Listen, Reb Mordkhe, who says that Rubin, Simon, and Levi from the Gemara are the same people you are talking about? In the Gemara they talk about Rubin the woodcutter, about Simon the shoemaker, and Levi the water carrier." Reb Mordkhe left him a very satisfied man. He lit his pipe and coughed a bit and felt very pleased. I thought that Reb Moyshele was a good teacher. He said that Rubin was a woodcutter, Simon a shoemaker, and Levi a water carrier. So did I tell the truth? He was a good teacher.

Reb Mordkhe was also applying for tax-free loans. He was always ready for one. At the beginning of the summer, he was always short of money to buy an orchard. "I am such a *meivn*," he used to say. "In order to make it work, I need to earn a large fortune. I will not only be able to repay the loan but I will have a little left over as well." That was what he thought at the beginning of each summer. After the summer, it turned out that he had made a mistake and saved nothing for the orchard. He needed to begin again with a tax-free loan.

The moon rose higher in the sky. The little town begins to emerge from the fog of darkness. The market place is lit up. From the street that opens on to the door of Piotrikowsky house and leads to the market place, emerge two Strzegowo businessmen. One of them goes toward the Mlawa road, near his own home. Reb Israel Rosen, he walks not with long but with rather quick steps. A good-looking man with a long beard that, because of the wind, twirls around on each of his cheeks. He is in deep thought and singing to himself a *khsidic* tune. Who knows if the tempo of the tune goes hand-in-hand with his thoughts?

A complicated type, not always sure of what he thinks, a type who is different from everyone else with all his many interests, Reb Zalman Davidowich. A man with a special sense of humor, he figures out Reb Israel's deals – an orchard, a house, a dog, a table in the market place, a place to make *kvass*. So he is sometimes known as Israel, the Kvassnik. And who doesn't remember the blond, Shmuel Yazover, who was the *shamis* and who went around to remind people about *slikhis*, banging on the windows: "Reb Israel Kvassnik, wake up for *slikhis*!"

Before Zalman departed for his pilgrimage, he thought about his leaving. And his life was full of many colors. In short, one could talk to him about many different subjects. Suddenly he becomes very outspoken, not choosing his words carefully and not paying attention to whom he is speaking. At certain times, when he was very upset one could get an answer like, "Go hit your head against the wall!" A very impulsive character, because of many different reasons, perhaps because he was not very free in his thoughts. He was very like quicksilver. A student of the Torah. He fought very stubbornly against Zionism. But as it has been recounted, in the ghetto he often spoke with great remorse about the monumental mistakes he had made. I'm not forgetting here how much I personally suffered his wrath because I was so strong a Zionist. And I remember very well that, although we were not very friendly, he came to see me the evening before I left for Palestine, to say goodbye.

His partner was very different from Israel Rosen. He was shorter. Coming into the market place he turns first to the right and heads toward several houses, goes to a large one and checks to see if the lock is secured, then turns back several houses and walks up many stairs to his own home.

Reb Faivl Novogrodsky was one of the best types of people in Strzegowo. Perhaps it was because he was such a sick man. In the last years he was very ill and his whole life was determined by it from one attack to the next – it was mostly heart trouble. One could see him running from a long distance away. In between he studied a few sentences and took part in the community discussions. Why does he remain in my memory as a sick man? Perhaps it is because of the characteristic way he spoke to me in the midst of his illness.

"Reb Faivil," I used to ask him, "What is missing in your life?" And he answered, "Nothing is lacking and I have nothing." Two nights before he died I was sitting in his house. And when he came to himself after a while, he said: "What is your problem? Live, live while you are young." And a minute later: "Live, for you see what life is really about." A good person, a learned man, and with great courage. When sitting and studying a few lines, he could spend as much time as necessary – the longer it was the more satisfied he was. For years a worker in the community, he was beloved by the people. These two men, Faivl Novogrodsky and Israel Rosen, are coming from the home of Yitzkhak Meir Piotrikowsky. Every evening they enjoy themselves in the office over a few lines of Gemara and a tasty glass of tea. Then they talk about many different issues, in general as well as personal ones. Reb Moyshe Shoykhet, in the sharpness of his insight calls the little table around which the three sit the "mysterious table" because they place there every secret in Strzegowo.

The second door of the same house leads to Piotrikowsky's mill. The door reminds me of a remarkable person in Strzegowo, an interesting type who, one could say, was not recognized in a tragic way. It was Saul David Tshizik. I'm reminded of an episode that left a deep imprint on me. Our house was a central place for political news. My father was one of the first subscribers to a newspaper called "The Friend." People liked to hear the news. One night Saul David Tshizik was in our house. He sat talking to my father for a few hours, and when he left late at night, my father said to my mother, "He is a man of the Enlightenment."

At that time, I didn't quite understand the meaning of the word, but it sounded to me somewhat mysterious. From that time on I looked at him with great respect. An intellectual! When I was a little older, I often had the opportunity to talk with him. I was very interested in what he had to say. Then I began to realize how far he was torn from his own self. A learned person in his own town of Plonsk, he seemed a good person who was drawn to intellectual issues. In those years Plonsk was deeply inspired by the spirit of the enlightenment and Zionism. If he had stayed there or left for another place with a similar atmosphere, he would have lived freely in his striving. He was neither a strong type nor a revolutionary one, it seemed, so he was not recognized by those around him or by his family.

I can see him now, standing in the house of study, bent over a book which he held near his face. Soon he took the ends of his beard in his mouth and continued to look into the book, totally absorbed and interested. When he had some free time he liked to go into the fields near the river and think. He often gazed at a book that he continually read. What are you reading? Frishman, David Frishman. A Gentile he was – who doesn't remember him from those times? From then, there remained the Stories from Plonsk, like "Yizkor" and "The Travels of Copernicus." And what's that – Yehuda Leib Gordon. He knew many stories and poems.

That's the way he used to get involved and suddenly start thinking and become silent. That way he went back in his thoughts about ten years and was completely absorbed. Who knows. He was a tragic figure but an interesting one.

From the stairs looking across the market emerges a tall man, an old one with a white beard, closes the cover of his spice-holder, puts the key in the lock, and waits until his wife says, "Stop!" That means she has already locked the door from within. For a man of his age it was already time for him to go to bed. This is Elye Leib Eidlitz. Who couldn't identify him – the deacon of the community's cemetery society, or as he was often called, the Expeditor. That's the way he went around the town. Nothing special, just a normal, gray life – praying, eating, sleeping, from time to time catching up with a little gossip. But whenever there was a catastrophe of any sort in the town, when someone died, for example, then he was revitalized. There suddenly was a sparkle in his eyes and he seemed on the whole to get younger. Then was the time for him to get ready to do his work: first to prepare the grave, then to start dealing with the members of the burial committee. To the young ones, he detailed the ordinary work, like calling the others, and drawing water for their tasks. Then it was necessary to get the shroud sewn, to see that the boards for the coffin were cut. For every task he was careful to use special language that was required to get the work done. For example, the word "good" was never allowed to be used. It's a funeral for a dead person – how can you say, "good?" Instead one only used the word, "right." The corpse was measured with a white thread – right. The measurements of the coffin were worked out – right. The shroud was sewn according to plan – right. The grave was correctly dug – right. There was plenty to do at the graveyard. Who should take the corpse down from the wagon? Who should do other arrangements? Who should say the prayer when the body is interred in the grave? And then he alone went into the grave, crouched on his knees and looked over the coffin to see that nothing was placed incorrectly as the corpse was covered with the special cloth. Then he began to say his own version of the prayers. Like a real craftsman he put together leaves and twigs and then placed them on the eyes and mouth of the corpse, asked for forgiveness, and covered the corpse again. Then he uncovered the hands of the corpse and placed some twigs in them, bent the head of the corpse away from the direction of the town, and then said the final prayers. And standing nearby, I gave thanks that Elye Leib brought all the dead of the town to the cemetery.

But not only during catastrophes was Elye Leib made happy. He was after all the head of the funeral committee, a group that was committed to bringing the dead to glory. Just this group that took care of all crises and occurrences, the ones whose job it was to send people off on their last journeys, without a thought of making a penny. And in coming into contact with the dead, he developed a special attitude toward life: "No one lives forever, so why is there egoism?" And the person who died was exalted. And though all the members of the committee came into contact with the dead, Elye was nevertheless the head of the group. And he always had the opportunity to think of his duties without the other concerns of the group. The rules of his duty were written in a black book bound with gold letters and kept at his home. On the pages of his records the names of the committee were written. The rest of the book smelled of the other world. There were indicated the "addresses" of those who died and were committed to the earth of the cemetery. Well, it's really a major question if Elye Leib himself found a place in the cemetery. No one ever discovered any references to him in the labyrinth of names and comments, written half in Yiddish and half in Hebrew.

I once was given the task by Elye Leib of checking the names of the dead. Then I realized why so many gravesites were misplaced. There were two worlds there – in the cemetery the dead were buried, but their addresses were written in this book.

Not only the records reminded Elye Leib of his position. But there were also many days of memory [the yearly observances] that were days of celebration for the members of the burial committee. For a few days earlier, Elye Leib was occupied. He was concerned with cakes and brandy.

Before the holidays, the young men used to go out and collect candles. In the evening the house of study was lit up with all those lights. The place took on a special meaning. Everything was covered with light and the members felt joyful, saying prayers in raised voices all the night through till the next morning when they all began to pray, everyone being present. And when they were done all went to Elye Leib's house for the conclusion of their prayers. Who then could compare himself with Elye Leib?

The second big party took place at Yitzkhak Meir Piotrikowsky's on Simkhas Torah when the beginning of the Torah is read. It made an imposing picture. People from all walks of life sat around the tables at Piotrikowsky's place. It was symbolic of the whole town – the brotherhood, the concern of the people one for another, was revealed in that holiday celebration. There was no separation between believers and non-believers, between the poor and the rich, between scholars and ordinary people, between merchants and wagon handlers. All were members of the burial society. All met with one object, which made no distinction between classes and trades. What made it happen was death. And therefore on the greatest holiday for Jews, Simkhas Torah, all should enjoy equally without any distinction at all.

Time passes slowly, and life, little by little, takes on new forms. The young people were concerned with many different things – new organizations, Zionism, and the land of Israel. The young men no longer went around collecting candles to light the House of Study, which became just a memory of the former good times. For Itche Meir Piotrikowsky there were also many changes. Children grew up and often married away from home. A part of the house was taken over by Piotrikowsky's son, Anshl, and many other rooms were modernized. The old-fashioned furniture was replaced by new pieces that seemed to stand on chicken-thin feet. The floors no longer shone as earlier. And on one Simkhas Torah the members of the burial society looked crossly at the fact that the furniture seemed different and the floors were becoming shoddy.

Once during Simkhas Torah his wife, Khanele, said to him:

"Itche Meir, the house is falling apart!" Itche Meir became pale and answered, "Better it should be that way when the members of the burial committee come than something worse. . . ." But the members of the committee no longer came to his house. That same winter he died in Warsaw at the wedding of his first grandchild.

JOSEPH ROSENBERG

Zuhg Nit Keynmuhl

WORDS: HIRSH GLIK   MUSIC: FROM A MELODY BY POKRAS

Zuhg nit keynmuhl az du geist dem letstn veg,
Ven himlen blaiene farshteln bloye teg;
Vail kumen vet nuhch undzer oysgebenkte shuh,
Es vet a poyk ton undzer truht: mir zainen duh!

Never say that you have reached the very end,
Though leaden skies a bitter future may portend;
Because the hour for which we yearn shall yet arrive
And our marching steps shall thunder: We survive!

From land of palm trees to the distant lands of snow,
We are here with our pain and our woe,
And everywhere our blood has fallen on the ground,
There our courage and our spirit shall rebound.

This song was written with our blood and not with lead;
It's not a song of birds that carol overhead.
It was a people midst the burning fires of hell.
That sang this song with gun in hand until they fell.

First written as the song of the Vilna ghetto, "Zuhg Nit Keynmuhl"
quickly became the anthem of all partisan groups.

Glossary

bankes. Small glass bulbs applied to the back or chest for treatment of colds

batkhen. Entertainer who performs at weddings and other occasions

bruder-keiver. Communal grave

felsher. A lay surgeon, capable of applying bankes

Gemara. A portion of the Talmud

khale. Soft, white bread often braided and made for the Sabbath

kheder. An elementary school

khoomits. Leavened bread

khsidim. (Sing. khusid) Orthodox Jews

kvass. A barley beer

landslait. Townspeople

matzo. Unleavened bread, eaten on Passover

meivn. Specialist, expert

minyan. Ten male Jews required for many rituals

Mishna. A section of the Talmud

mikve. A ritual bathhouse

rebitsn. The wife of the rabbi or a devout woman

Sabras. Native born Israelis; the term refers to a cactus

Shabis. The Sabbath

shamis. A deacon in the synagogue

shmalts. Rendered chicken fat

shoykhet. A person authorized to slaughter chickens and other meat

Simkhas Torah. A holiday celebrating a reading of the beginning of the Torah

slikhis. Holiday services

tsholnt. A casserole placed in the oven on Friday since it's forbidden to cook on the Sabbath